# Grammar Network

コミュニケーションにリンクする英文法

Hiromi Akimoto | Mayumi Hamada

Australia · Brazil · Mexico · Singapore · United Kingdom · United States

**Grammar Network**

**Hiromi Akimoto / Mayumi Hamada**

© 2019 Cengage Learning K.K.

ALL RIGHTS RESERVED. No part of this work covered by the copyright herein may be reproduced, transmitted, stored, or used in any form or by any means—graphic, electronic, or mechanical, including but not limited to photocopying, recording, scanning, digitizing, taping, Web distribution, information networks, or information storage and retrieval systems—without the prior written permission of the publisher.

"National Geographic," "National Geographic Society" and the Yellow Border Design are registered trademarks of the National Geographic Society ® Marcas Registradas

**Photo Credits:**
Cover: © Henrik Sorensen/DigitalVision/Getty Images
p. 8: © Fascinadora/iStock.com; p. 12: © Rauluminate/iStock.com; p. 16: © Archive Photos/Moviepix/Getty Images; p. 20: © Alamy (RM)/Pacific Press Service; p. 24: © anyaberkut/iStock.com; p. 28: © Rolls Press/Popperfoto/Getty Images; p. 32: © DGLimages/iStock.com; p. 36: © jacoblund/iStock.com; p. 40: © kimberrywood/iStock.com; p. 44: © monkeybusinessimages/iStock.com; p. 48: © dennisvdw/iStock.com; p. 52: © Jupiterimages/Stockbyte/Getty Images; p. 56: © liza5450/iStock.com; p. 60: © Christopher Robbins/DigitalVision/Getty Images; p. 64: (t) © GetUpStudio/iStock.com, (b) © DestinoIkigai/iStock.com; p. 68: © martin-dm/iStock.com; p. 72: © SerrNovik/iStock.com; p. 76: © Alamy (RM)/Pacific Press Service; p. 80: © LisaValder/iStock.com; p. 84: © fizkes/iStock.com

For permission to use material from this textbook or product, e-mail to **eltjapan@cengage.com**

ISBN: 978-4-86312-348-9

**National Geographic Learning | Cengage Learning K.K.**
No. 2 Funato Building 5th Floor
1-11-11 Kudankita, Chiyoda-ku
Tokyo 102-0073
Japan

Tel: 03-3511-4392
Fax: 03-3511-4391

# はしがき

　皆さんはこれまで英語を学ぶ過程において英文法の知識を吸収してきていますが、文法事項を理解して定着させるのに苦労した人もいるのではないでしょうか。また、関係代名詞や仮定法過去などの難解な文法用語を目にして、英語そのものが嫌になった人も少なくないのではないかと思います。あるいは、せっかく英文法を習ったのに、実際のコミュニケーションの場面で使う機会がないまま、単なる知識で終わってしまい残念に感じている人もいるかもしれません。

　本書は、文法事項を整理して学び直すことと、これまで知識として蓄えてきた英文法をコミュニケーションで使える道具に転換することを目的に作られました。国内外での生活で外国の方と英語でコミュニケーションをとる際に必要な文法の知識を、さまざまなエクササイズを通して学べるようになっています。例文もなるべく平易で、かつ実際の会話で使われるような内容を扱っています。また、文法事項を使えるようにするだけでなく、リスニング力やライティング力も強化できるような構成を心がけました。

　海外のみならず国内でも、これからますます英語による対人コミュニケーションの必要性が高まってくるものと思われます。そのための準備として本書をご利用いただき、役に立つことができればとても嬉しく思います。英文法が苦手で英語嫌いの人でも、本書を通して今までと違った角度から英文法を楽しく学び直し、苦手意識を持たずに英語を使うことができるようになることを願っています。

　最後になりましたが、本書の完成まで丁寧なアドバイスでご尽力いただきましたナショナルジオグラフィック ラーニングの吉田剛氏に感謝を申し上げます。

稻本浩美<br>濱田真由美

# Contents

はしがき　　　　　　　　　　3
本書の構成と使い方　　　　　6
音声ファイルの利用方法　　　7

## BASIC

**Unit 1** Just one bottle of orange juice —— 8
名詞

**Unit 2** I major in business —— 12
be 動詞と一般動詞

**Unit 3** Only on special occasions —— 16
前置詞

**Unit 4** I want to buy T-shirts or caps —— 20
接続詞

**Unit 5** I'm checking a flight schedule —— 24
時制①：現在形と現在進行形

**Unit 6** He led a huge march in Washington, D.C. —— 28
時制②：過去形と現在完了形

**Unit 7** What are you going to do? —— 32
時制③：未来形

**Unit 8** Can I have a single room tonight? —— 36
助動詞①：can / may

**Unit 9** That would be the perfect thing to do —— 40
助動詞②：could / would

**Unit 10** Do I have to sign up for the lesson? —— 44
助動詞③：should / must / have to / had better

| Unit | Title | Topic | Page |
|---|---|---|---|
| Unit 11 | I got fascinated with the beauty of the town | 受動態 | 48 |
| Unit 12 | Did you bring anything to eat? | 不定詞①：基本用法 | 52 |
| Unit 13 | It's the most popular restaurant | 比較 | 56 |
| Unit 14 | The guy who moved next door is very strange | 関係詞①：関係代名詞 | 60 |
| Unit 15 | If you were me, where would you go? | 仮定法①：仮定法過去 | 64 |

## PLUS

| Unit | Title | Topic | Page |
|---|---|---|---|
| Unit 16 | My hobby is playing sports | 動名詞 | 68 |
| Unit 17 | I'm too excited to sleep tonight | 不定詞②：応用構文と原形不定詞 | 72 |
| Unit 18 | I watched a very exciting movie | 分詞 | 76 |
| Unit 19 | That's where I was born | 関係詞②：関係副詞 | 80 |
| Unit 20 | I shouldn't have done such a stupid thing | 仮定法②：仮定法過去完了 | 84 |

More Tips for Grammar & Pair Practice　　88

# 本書の構成と使い方

本書は、基礎編（BASIC）15ユニットと応用編（PLUS）5ユニットの計20ユニットで構成されています。また、巻末には各ユニットの「詳しい文法説明」と「コミュニカティブなアクティビティ」を収録しています。

**各ユニットの構成と使い方**
各ユニットは4ページ構成で、各ページの内容および使い方は次のとおりです。

### 1ページ目

**Dialogue**　文法事項を含む会話

ユニットで取り上げられている文法事項に該当する部分を青色で示しています。音声を何度か聞いて会話練習をしましょう。

**Warm Up**　Dialogueのリスニング内容把握問題

Dialogueに関する英文を聞いたあと、Dialogueの内容に合っているかどうかを答えます。

### 2ページ目

**▶Tips for Grammar◀**　文法事項説明

ユニットで取り上げられている文法事項のうち、特に押さえてほしいポイントに絞って簡潔に説明しています。

**Practice 1**　文法問題1

Tips for Grammarで扱われている文法事項に関する問題です。

### 3ページ目

**Practice 2**　文法問題2

イラストを見ながら、（　）に適語を入れて英文を完成させる問題です。解答後、音声を聞いて答えをチェックします。巻末の**More Tips for Grammar**も参考にしてください。

**Practice 3**　文法問題3

いろいろな形式で出題されます。解答後、音声を聞いて答えをチェックします。巻末の**More Tips for Grammar**も参考にしてください。

4ページ目

**Practice 4**　　ライティング問題

ユニットで取り上げられている文法事項を使いながら、自分のことについて書いて紹介する問題です。

**Practice 5**　　スピーキング練習

Practice 4 で書いたことをクラスメートとシェアするコミュニカティブなスピーキング活動です。

▶ **Grammar in Action** ◀　文法事項に関する補足説明やコラム

ユニットで取り上げられている文法事項が、日常会話や歌、映画のシーンなどで実際にどのように使われているかを紹介しています。

## 巻末の More Tips for Grammar & Pair Practice について

各ユニット見開き 2 ページ構成で、各ページの基本的な内容と使い方は次のとおりです。

左ページ　▶ **More Tips for Grammar** ◀

Tips for Grammar の詳しい説明です。Practice 2 と 3 を解答する際に参考にしてください。

右ページ　**Pair Practice**

ユニットで学習した文法事項を定着させるためのスピーキング練習です。ペアやグループで取り組める楽しいアクティビティが紹介されています。

### 音声ファイルの利用方法

https://ngljapan.com/gramnetwork-audio/

 のアイコンがある箇所の音声ファイルにアクセスできます。

❶ 上記 URL にアクセス、または QR コードをスマートフォンなどのリーダーでスキャン
❷ 希望の番号をクリックして音声ファイルをダウンロードまたは再生

# BASIC

# Just one bottle of orange juice

Unit 1

名詞

## Dialogue A-02

青色部分に注意しながら会話を聞いてみましょう。

Bob: I'll go grocery shopping this afternoon. Do you need anything?
Ai: Oh, good. Can you buy some orange juice? Well, just one bottle of that.
Bob: OK, anything else?
Ai: I also want a can of tomato soup.
Bob: Is that all?
Ai: Well, ah... actually I also need a carton of eggs, and three pieces of cheesecake.
Bob: Wow. That's a lot!
Ai: Sorry. I'll pay you later.

## Warm Up 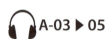A-03 ▶ 05

英文を聞いて、ダイアログの内容と一致する場合は T を、一致しない場合は F を ○ で囲みましょう。

1. T / F
2. T / F
3. T / F

Unit 1  Just one bottle of orange juice

## ▶ Tips for Grammar ◀　名詞

### 数えられる名詞 VS. 数えられない名詞

名詞には数えられる名詞と数えられない名詞があり、辞書の中ではそれぞれ C 、 U と表記されています。リンゴやオレンジは一つ一つ数えることができますが、一定の形を持たないコーヒーや紅茶、ワイン、砂糖などは、容器に入っていないかぎりは数えられません。パン、チーズ、紙、布、お金、髪の毛、家具（furniture）、荷物（baggage）などは日本語の概念では数えられそうですが、英語の場合は数えられません。数えられない名詞に単数を表す a/an や複数を表す -s/-es などがつくことはなく、some ...、a lot of ...、a piece of ...、a cup of ...、a can of ...、a bowl of ...、a bottle of ...、a head of ... などの表現が使われます。

 I bought an apple and three oranges.　私はリンゴ1個とオレンジ3個を買った。
 I ate three pieces of French bread.　私はフランスパンを3切れ食べた。

### 集合名詞

family（家族）、class（クラス）、group（集団）のように何人かの人々の集合体は集合名詞と呼ばれ、その意味合いに応じて単数形、複数形の使い分けがなされます。

 My family are all baseball fans.　私の家族はみんな野球ファンだ。
 Three families are on the boat.　3組の家族がそのボートに乗っている。

⇒詳しくは **88** ページ参照

## Practice 1

英文中で間違いのある部分に下線を引き、適切な形に訂正しましょう。

1. I usually eat two breads and an orange every morning.

2. The police is still looking for the criminal.

3. My mother bought a wine for my father's birthday.

4. I have two baggages to check in.

5. I usually wear contact lens, not glasses.

6. I need some white papers to make a photocopy.

# Practice 2  A-06     Hint p. 88

下の英文はイラストを描写しています。（ ）に適切な語を入れ、音声を聞いて答えを確認しましょう。

1. Ai has beautiful (　　　　) (　　　　).
2. Bob wants to have (　　　　) (　　　　) (　　　　) (　　　　).
3. Lisa needs to buy (　　　　) (　　　　) (　　　　) (　　　　).
4. There (　　　　) a lot of (　　　　) in my sister's room.

# Practice 3  A-07 ▶ 11     Hint p. 88

音声を聞いて（ ）に適切な語を入れましょう。

1. Could you lend me (　　　　) (　　　　)?
2. Can I have (　　　　) (　　　　) (　　　　) water?
3. Can you go buy three (　　　　) (　　　　) (　　　　)?
4. I really want to have another (　　　　) (　　　　) (　　　　).
5. I want to order (　　　　) (　　　　) (　　　　) tomato soup.

# Practice 4

あなたは友人と2人でレストランに来ています。次のメニューをもとに、下の例を参考にしながら、自分が食べたいものをオーダーするときの文を書いてみましょう。

| Menu at Deep Blue Sea ||||
|---|---|---|---|
| **Appetizers** | | **Drinks** | |
| Onion soup | (cup) $4.00  (bowl) $5.00 | Coffee | (cup) $3.00  (pot) $5.00 |
| Clam chowder | (cup) $4.00  (bowl) $5.00 | Tea | (cup) $3.00  (pot) $5.00 |
| Caesar salad | (small bowl) $7.50 | Coke | $5.00 |
| | (large bowl) $9.50 | Orange juice | $6.00 |
| Seafood salad | (small bowl) $8.00 | Apple juice | $6.00 |
| | (large bowl) $10.00 | | |
| **Main Dish** | | **Desserts** | |
| BLT sandwich | $15.00 | Gelato | $6.00 |
| Roast beef sandwich | $17.00 | Apple pie | (small piece) $4.00 |
| Hamburger | $11.00 | | (large piece) $6.00 |
| Cheeseburger | $12.50 | Chocolate cake | (small piece) $4.00 |
| Pizza margherita | $13.00 | | (large piece) $6.00 |
| Pepperoni pizza | $13.50 | | |

For an appetizer, I'd like a bowl of clam chowder. And for the main dish, I'd like to have a BLT sandwich. For dessert, I'll have a small piece of chocolate cake and a cup of tea.

# Practice 5

クラスメートとPractice 4の答えをシェアしましょう。

▶ **Grammar in Action** ◀   コーヒーの注文の仕方は？

コーヒーや紅茶は数えられない名詞ですが、レストランで注文する際は具体的な1つのメニューとして考えるので、数えられる名詞扱いとなることもあります。正確には "We'd like to have three cups of coffee and two cups of tea." ですが、実際には "Three coffees and two teas, please." のようになります。

# BASIC

## Unit 2: I major in business

**be 動詞と一般動詞**

### Dialogue  A-13

青色部分に注意しながら会話を聞いてみましょう。

Kaz: Hi! My name is Kazuki. Nice to meet you. Please call me Kaz.

Lisa: OK, Kaz. I'm Lisa. Nice to meet you, too. Are you from Japan?

Kaz: Yes. This is the first time for me to stay in a dorm in the U.S. I'm a little nervous.

Lisa: Oh, don't worry. Everyone in this dorm is very kind and friendly.

Kaz: I'm glad to hear that. What's your major, Lisa?

Lisa: I study biology, and I want to go to a medical school. How about you, Kaz?

Kaz: I major in business now. When I go back to my country, I want to start a trading business.

Lisa: That's good. I hope you have a great time here in the U.S.

Kaz: Thank you!

### Warm Up  A-14 ▶ 16

英文を聞いて、ダイアログの内容と一致する場合は T を、一致しない場合は F を○で囲みましょう。

1. T / F
2. T / F
3. T / F

Unit 2　I major in business

## ▶ Tips for Grammar ◀　動詞

### be 動詞
be 動詞は、is、am、are などを指します。主語と名詞もしくは形容詞の間に be 動詞を置くことによって、be 動詞の前と後ろの語句をイコールの関係で結び付ける働きをします。また、否定文を作るには be 動詞の後に not を入れ、疑問文を作るには be 動詞を文頭に持ってきます。

　　I am a university student.　私は大学生だ。

　　Are you an exchange student?　あなたは交換留学生なの？

　　Joe isn't a freshman.　ジョーは大学1年生ではない。

### 一般動詞
一般動詞は「動き」を表す場合に使う動詞です。3 人称単数（he / she / it）が主語で現在の事柄を表す場合は原則として動詞に -s/-es をつけますが、疑問文と否定文の場合は does や doesn't が新たに加わることにより、動詞に -s/-es をつける必要がなくなります。

　　He goes to school every day but Sunday.　彼は日曜日以外は毎日学校に行く。

　　Does he live in the dorm?　彼は寮に住んでいるの？

　　She doesn't like mathematics.　彼女は数学が好きではない。

⇒ 詳しくは 90 ページ参照

# Practice 1

英文中の be 動詞や一般動詞に下線を引きましょう。次に、その英文を疑問文と否定文にしましょう。

1. Kyoto is one of the famous sightseeing spots in Japan.

　　疑問文⇒

　　否定文⇒

2. Joe wants to be a doctor.

　　疑問文⇒

　　否定文⇒

3. Kaz and Yuki are in New York now.

　　疑問文⇒

　　否定文⇒

4. Her parents want her to study abroad.

　　疑問文⇒

　　否定文⇒

# Practice 2

下の英文はイラストを描写しています。（　）に適切な語を入れ、音声を聞いて答えを確認しましょう。

1. Bob (　　　) a college student and (　　　) (　　　).
2. Rika and Rumi (　　　) friends and they (　　　) toy dolls.
3. Kaz (　　　) a kind boy. He always (　　　) (　　　) in need.
4. Ai (　　　) (　　　) and comic books.

# Practice 3

次の英文に間違いがあれば、その部分に下線を引いて訂正し、音声を聞いて答えを確認しましょう。

1. I don't want to marry with my boyfriend now.

2. I need to discuss about this matter with you.

3. Do I have to attend the meeting?

4. Please enter into the room quietly.

5. Don't approach to the building.

# Practice 4

下の例を参考にしながら、次の 1 ～ 3 に関する自分の情報を枠内の英文の（ ）に入れて、自己紹介文を完成させましょう。

1. 名前とニックネーム、出身地、所属
2. 趣味や好きなこと
3. これからやってみたいこと

例

Hello. My name is ( Kazuki ). Please call me ( Kaz ). I'm from ( Osaka, Japan ) and am a ( university student ). I ( major in business ) and I will ( study Economics ) here. I like ( watching baseball games ). I also like ( watching American movies ) and ( listening to American music ). I want to ( visit many places in the U.S. such as the Niagara Falls, New York City, and Los Angeles ).

| Hello. My name is ( ). Please call me ( ). I'm from ( ) and am a ( ). I ( ) and I will ( ) here. I like ( ). I want to ( ). |
|---|

# Practice 5

クラスメートと Practice 4 の答えをシェアしましょう。

▶ **Grammar in Action** ◀　いろいろな意味を持つ便利な一般動詞の have

初対面ではまず互いに名乗り合う場合が多いので、"What is your name?" と尋ねる頻度はそれほど高くありません。この質問文の場合は be 動詞である is を使って尋ねていますが、一般動詞 have を使って "May I have your name, please?" と言うと、より丁寧な尋ね方になります。have は便利な動詞で、"I'll have this one."（こちらをいただきます）のように買い物をする際にも使えます。

# Only on special occasions

Unit 3

前置詞

## Dialogue   A-20

青色部分に注意しながら会話を聞いてみましょう。

Ai: I watched the movie *Roman Holiday* yesterday. Have you ever seen it before?

Bob: Oh, yes. It was great. Did you watch it on DVD at home?

Ai: Yeah. Since the movie was released in the 50's, I didn't expect it to be good. But I really liked it. I don't feel it's old-fashioned at all!

Bob: I agree. Well, I like the scene where Joe and Ann get on a scooter in the city of Rome.

Ai: I remember that. How about Ann's haircut? Wasn't she so cute in her short hair?

Bob: That's true. What do you think the best scenes of the movie were?

Ai: I liked the one where Ann put her hand in the Mouth of Truth.

Bob: Right. I also like the scene where Ann is eating gelato on the Spanish Steps.

## Warm Up  A-21 ▶ 23

英文を聞いて、ダイアログの内容と一致する場合はTを、一致しない場合はFを○で囲みましょう。

1. T / F
2. T / F
3. T / F

Unit 3　Only on special occasions

## ▶ Tips for Grammar ◀　前置詞

### 「時」と「場所」を表す at、in、on
前置詞 at、in、on には様々な用法があります。ここでは「時」と「場所」を表す使い方を確認しましょう。

Paul arrived **at** the church.　ポールは教会に到着した。　［場所］
The next class begins **at** 10:40.　次の授業は 10 時 40 分に始まる。　［時］
I met my old friend **in** the movie theater.　映画館で旧友に会った。　［場所］
I made a trip to New York **in** 1992.　私は 1992 年にニューヨークへ旅行した。　［時］
The book **on** the desk is not mine.　机の上の本は私のものではない。　［場所］
Let's eat out **on** Christmas.　クリスマスには外食しよう。　［時］

### その他の用法
at、in、on には上記以外に次のような使い方もあります。

The gentleman **in** a pink shirt was looking for you.　ピンクのシャツを着た男性が君を探していたよ。
I got **on** a bus but he rode **in** a taxi to get there.　そこへ行くのに私はバスに乗ったが、彼はタクシーに乗った。

⇒ 詳しくは **92** ページ参照

## Practice 1

英文中で間違いのある部分に下線を引き、適切な形に訂正しましょう。

1. I will arrive in the station at 10:00.

2. Why don't we go to the shrine at New Year's Day?

3. The next movie starts at 13:45 on that movie theater.

4. I left my cell phone at the table in the cafeteria.

5. John stayed at New Zealand twice in 1992.

6. I met my teacher on the department store on Sunday last week.

7. Look at the beautiful painting at the wall.

# Practice 2  A-24　　　　　　　　　　　　Hint p. 92

下の英文はイラストを描写しています。（　）に適切な語を入れ、音声を聞いて答えを確認しましょう。

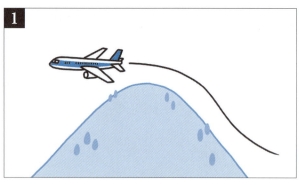

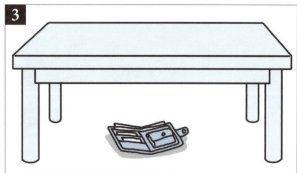

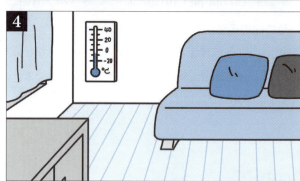

1. The airplane is flying (　　　　) the (　　　　).
2. There are beautiful stars (　　　　) the (　　　　).
3. The wallet is (　　　　) the (　　　　).
4. The temperature of this room (　　　　)(　　　　) zero.

# Practice 3  A-25　　　　　　　　　　　　Hint p. 92

（　）に適切な前置詞を入れ、音声を聞いて答えを確認しましょう。

1. I was waiting (　　　　) him (　　　　) the bus stop.
2. It takes about 11 hours (　　　　) Tokyo (　　　　) New York by plane.
3. Kana left (　　　　) Italy last month.
4. She is my neighbor. Her room is next (　　　　) mine in the dorm.
5. The key was (　　　　) my mother's bag, so I couldn't find it.

# Practice 4

下の日記の例を参考にしながら、次の点に関する自分の情報を枠内の英文の（　）に入れて、休日をどのように過ごしたかを述べる文を完成させましょう。

- 何時に起きたか
- 誰とどこへ行ったか
- それはどこにあるのか
- どのお店で何を買ったのか
- どこで何を食べたのか
- その後、何をしたのか

例

I woke up at ( 8:30 ) on ( Sunday ).
I went to ( a newly opened department store ) with ( my friend, Kathy ).
It is located next to ( the East Coast Plaza in the downtown area ).
I bought ( a hat and a winter jacket ) at ( XYZ Mart ).
I ate ( a ham and cheese sandwich ) in a restaurant named ( One Tree Top ).
Then we ( visited A to Z travel to book airplane tickets for Australia ).

---

I woke up at (　　　) on (　　　).
I went to (　　　) with (　　　).
It is located (　　　).
I bought (　　　) at (　　　).
I ate (　　　) in a restaurant named (　　　).
Then we (　　　).

---

# Practice 5

クラスメートと Practice 4 の答えをシェアしましょう。

▶ **Grammar in Action** ◀　特定の日を表す on

Dialogue に出てきた映画『ローマの休日』の中で、「昼食にシャンパンを飲むなんてなかなかの暮らしぶりだね」とジョー（グレゴリー・ペック）に言われたアン（オードリー・ヘプバーン）は "Only on special occasions."「特別な時だけよ」と返します。このように、on は特定の日を表す際にも使われます。

# BASIC

# I want to buy T-shirts or caps

Unit 4

接続詞

## Dialogue  A-27

青色部分に注意しながら会話を聞いてみましょう。

Kaz: Excuse me. I want to buy T-shirts or caps as souvenirs for my friends. Where can I find them?
Clerk: Well, you can go to the Market Place. Go straight for four blocks and cross Mission Street. And then you can...
Kaz: Ah... Wait. Go straight for four blocks and cross...
Clerk: Mission Street. After you cross it, you'll see the Market Place on your right. Although it's a small building, you can't miss it because it has a big pink sign.
Kaz: Thank you. Is it far from here? I've been walking all day and I'm very tired.
Clerk: It's just a 10-minute walk, so don't worry! But you can take a bus right over there, if you like.

## Warm Up  A-28 ▶ 30

英文を聞いて、ダイアログの内容と一致する場合はTを、一致しない場合はFを○で囲みましょう。

1. T / F
2. T / F
3. T / F

Unit 4　I want to buy T-shirts or caps

## ▶ Tips for Grammar ◀　接続詞

**よく使われる接続詞**

接続詞は単語と単語、節と節、そして文と文をつなぐ役割を果たします。使用頻度の高い接続詞には次のようなものがあります。普段は意識せずに使うことが多いのですが、会話の流れをスムーズにしたり文脈を理解しやすくしたりする働きもありますから、よく確認しておきましょう。

John **and** Paul sing together in the band.　ジョンとポールはバンドで一緒に歌っている。

Would you like tea **or** coffee?　紅茶かコーヒーをいかがですか。

I want to go driving, **but** it's raining.　ドライブに行きたいけど雨が降っている。

I sent the present by sea mail **because** it was cheaper.　（船便だと）より安いのでプレゼントを船便で送った。

**After** shopping, we went to a restaurant.　買い物のあと、私たちはレストランに行った。

**Although** he is only three, he can read.　彼はわずか3歳なのに字が読める。

⇒ 詳しくは **94** ページ参照

## Practice 1

（　）に入る適切な接続詞を枠内から選んで記入しましょう。それぞれ1回しか使えません。

| and | because | before | but |
|-----|---------|--------|-----|
| or  | so      | while  |     |

1. This PC is very small, (　　　　) it is easy to carry.
2. She is going to the cafeteria, (　　　　) I'm not going today.
3. Kaz was doing his homework (　　　　) his roommate was sleeping.
4. We finished lunch (　　　　) went shopping.
5. Which would you prefer, a window seat (　　　　) an aisle seat?
6. He got an excellent grade (　　　　) he worked very hard.
7. Make sure to turn off the light (　　　　) you leave the room.

# Practice 2

 A-31   p. 94

下の英文はイラスト内に矢印で示した人物のセリフです。(　)に適切な語を入れ、音声を聞いて答えを確認しましょう。

1. Do you want to (　　　　) out (　　　　) (　　　　) pizza?
2. Turn off your phone (　　　　) the test (　　　　).
3. We can't go hiking (　　　　) (　　　　) (　　　　).
4. I need my (　　　　) and an (　　　　) (　　　　) to get on the plane.

# Practice 3

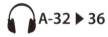 A-32 ▶ 36　　　　Hint p. 94

音声を聞いて (　) に適切な語を入れましょう。

1. (　　　) (　　　) (　　　) (　　　), I went to New York with my friends.
2. (　　　) (　　　) (　　　) (　　　), I stayed up late to finish my homework.
3. You can have a chance to try again, (　　　) (　　　) (　　　) (　　　).
4. Let's go on a vacation (　　　) (　　　) (　　　) (　　　) (　　　).
5. (　　　) (　　　) today, (　　　) why don't we go to the pool?

# Practice 4

例を参考にしながら、自分が朝起きてから出かけるまでの行動について述べる枠内の文を完成させましょう。

例

**When** I wake up, first I ( go to the bathroom ).
**Then**, I ( take a shower and get dressed ).
**After that**, I ( drink coffee and eat a piece of toast ).
**Then**, I ( brush my teeth ).
**And then**, I ( check text messages on my cell phone ).
**Before** I leave home, I ( look in the mirror and check how I look ).

| |
|---|
| When I wake up, first I ( ). |
| Then, I ( ). |
| After that, I ( ). |
| Then, I ( ). |
| And then, I ( ). |
| Before I leave home, I ( ). |

# Practice 5

クラスメートと Practice 4 の答えをシェアしましょう。

---

▶ **Grammar in Action** ◀　対比の and

2つ以上のものを比べて述べたり、対になっているものを結びつけたりするときに and がよく使われます。皆さんの好きな洋楽の歌詞にも and がたくさん使われていますね。ジョン・レノンの "Happy Xmas (War Is Over)" という曲の中では、"the old and the young"（お年寄りに若い人たち）、"for weak and for strong"（弱き者も強き者も）、"for rich and the poor ones"（富める者も貧しき人も）というふうに、対になる語句が and で結ばれ効果的に使われています。

# BASIC

# I'm checking a flight schedule

**Unit 5**

時制①：現在形と現在進行形

## Dialogue  A-38

青色部分に注意しながら会話を聞いてみましょう。

Bob: Hi, Ai! You look busy. Are you writing a report?
Ai: No, I'm checking a flight schedule on the Internet. My sister is arriving from Japan tomorrow evening.
Bob: Really? That's exciting!
Ai: Yeah. She wants to go skiing at Greenmountain.
Bob: That's cool. Where else are you guys going?
Ai: Well, we are visiting New York City and attending the Times Square Countdown.
Bob: Wow, that's wonderful.
Ai: Yeah, I can't wait!

## Warm Up  A-39 ▶ 41

英文を聞いて、ダイアログの内容と一致する場合はTを、一致しない場合はFを○で囲みましょう。

1. T / F
2. T / F
3. T / F

Unit 5　I'm checking a flight schedule

## ▶ Tips for Grammar ◀　時制①

### 現在形
今の状態や現在における習慣を表す際に用います。

　He is a student at UCLA.　彼は UCLA の学生だ。

　I always drink coffee in the morning.　私はいつも朝にコーヒーを飲む。

### 現在進行形：《is / am / are + *doing*》
now や right now などとよく一緒に使われ、今まさに進行中の動作を表します。

　Rumi is drying her hair now.　ルミは今、髪の毛を乾かしている。

　Masaki is preparing for the test right now.　マサキはちょうど今、テストの準備をしているところだ。

### 頻度を表す副詞
以下の副詞はある事柄がどのくらいの頻度で起こるかを表していて、普通は現在形と共に用いられます。

| never | hardly | rarely | occasionally | sometimes | often | usually | always |
|---|---|---|---|---|---|---|---|
| 決して…ない | めったに…しない | まれにしか…しない | 時折 | ときどき | よく | 普通は | いつも |

頻度が低い ──────────────→ 頻度が高い

⇒ 詳しくは **96** ページ参照

# Practice 1

日本語をヒントにして、（　）に適切な語を入れましょう。

1. I (　　　　　) (　　　　　) to school.
   いつも歩いていく

2. John (　　　　　) (　　　　　) DVDs at home in his free time.
   たいてい見ている

3. My boyfriend and I (　　　　　) (　　　　　) driving on sunny days.
   よく行く

4. Rika (　　　　　) (　　　　　) dinner by herself.
   ときどき料理をする

5. I (　　　　　) (　　　　　) coffee at night.
   決して飲まない

25

# Practice 2  A-42  p. 96

下の英文はイラストを描写しています。（　）に適切な語を入れ、音声を聞いて答えを確認しましょう。

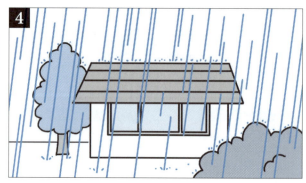

1. Lisa (　　　　) (　　　　) (　　　　) (　　　　) to her friend now.
2. Kaz (　　　　) (　　　　) (　　　　) three times a week.
3. These (　　　　) (　　　　) (　　　　) to Ai.
4. It (　　　　) (　　　　) now outside.

# Practice 3  A-43  p. 96

英文に間違いがあれば、その部分に下線を引いて訂正し、音声を聞いて答えを確認しましょう。

1. I am knowing that his story is not true.

2. Wait. I talk on the phone right now.

3. One of my friends is belonging to a baseball club.

4. Are you rarely remembering people's names?

5. Hey, don't disturb me. I do my homework now.

# Practice 4

スケジュール表の例を参考にして、自分自身の週間スケジュール表を作りましょう。次に、下の英文例を参考にしながら、頻度を表す副詞を使って自分のスケジュールを述べる文を書きましょう。

**例**

**My Weekly Schedule**

| Monday | Have 3 classes, lunch at a cafeteria, work part-time at a supermarket |
|---|---|
| Tuesday | Have 4 classes, bring a box lunch, go to a driving school |
| Wednesday | Have 3 classes, lunch at a cafeteria, go to a gym |
| Thursday | Have 4 classes, skip lunch, work part-time at a hamburger shop |
| Friday | Have 2 classes, bring a box lunch, go to a gym, watch a DVD at home |

A-44

I have three classes, and then work part-time at a supermarket on Monday. On Tuesday, I **always** bring my box lunch and I go to a driving school. After having three classes, I **sometimes** go to a gym on Wednesday. I **usually** skip lunch on Thursday. On Friday, I only have two classes and I **often** watch a DVD at home.

**My Weekly Schedule**

| Monday | |
|---|---|
| Tuesday | |
| Wednesday | |
| Thursday | |
| Friday | |

# Practice 5

クラスメートと Practice 4 の答えをシェアしましょう。

---

▶ **Grammar in Action** ◀　現在形で使う see、feel、know

96 ページにあるように、心理状態や感覚を表す動詞は通常、現在形で用います。映画『タイタニック』の主題歌である "My Heart Will Go On" の出だしでは、次のように現在形が使われています。

　"Every night in my dreams, I **see** you, I **feel** you. That is how I **know** you go on."
　(毎晩、私は夢の中であなたに会い、あなたのことを感じるのです。そんなふうにして、私にはあなたがどうしているかがわかるのです)

# BASIC

# He led a huge march in Washington, D.C.

Unit 6

時制②：過去形と現在完了形

## Dialogue  A-45

青色部分に注意しながら会話を聞いてみましょう。

Ai: What are you reading, Bob?

Bob: I'm reading a biography of...

Ai: Wait, let me guess who the person is. Give me a hint.

Bob: OK. He was born in Atlanta, Georgia in 1929. In 1963, he led a huge march in Washington, D.C. to support civil rights. And he gave his famous "I Have a Dream" speech to the crowd.

Ai: That's Martin Luther King, Jr! His speech has moved a lot of people's emotions in the world since then.

Bob: That's right. Although he was killed, his beliefs have been passed on to the next generation.

## Warm Up  A-46 ▶ 48

英文を聞いて、ダイアログの内容と一致する場合はTを、一致しない場合はFを○で囲みましょう。

1. T / F
2. T / F
3. T / F

28

Unit 6　He led a huge march in Washington, D.C.

## ▶Tips for Grammar◀　時制②

**過去形と現在完了形**

過去形は現在と切り離して過去のことだけを述べるのに使います。それに対して現在完了形は過去の出来事を現在と結び付けて説明する際に用います。

　　Rumi lost her credit card yesterday.　昨日、ルミはクレジットカードをなくした。
　　Rumi has lost her credit card.　ルミはクレジットカードをなくしてしまった。（今もまだ見つかっていない）

1つ目の例文では「ルミが昨日カードをなくした」という事実だけを伝えていて、そのカードがその後どうなったかは述べていません。2つ目の例文では「ルミが過去のある時点でカードをなくし、そのカードは今もまだ見つかっていない」という状況になります。

**現在完了形と時を表す副詞**

現在完了形は、過去からのつながりで現在の状況を述べるので、yesterday や last night、when 節など明らかに過去を表す表現と一緒に使うことはできません。

　　× They have arrived at the airport last night.
　　○ They arrived at the airport last night.　彼らは昨夜、空港に到着した。

**現在完了形と共によく使われる語**

現在完了形では for、since、once、twice、never、yet、already などの表現がよく使われます。

　　She has been sick since last Friday.　彼女は先週の金曜日から病気だ。
　　They have traveled in Europe twice.　彼らはヨーロッパを2回旅行したことがある。
　　I have already finished my homework.　私はもう宿題を終えた。

⇒詳しくは98ページ参照

# Practice 1

(　) の中から適切なほうを選び、完成した英文を日本語にしましょう。

1. I ( wanted / have wanted ) to be a doctor when I was a child.

2. Takashi ( visited / has visited ) London twice.

3. She ( decided / has decided ) to try painting when she was in junior high school.

4. Rika ( was / has been ) on a diet since she was 18.

5. Mike ( didn't go / hasn't gone ) shopping yet.

6. We ( lived / have lived ) in this city for more than 15 years.

# Practice 2  A-49  p. 98

下の英文はイラストを描写しています。（ ）に適切な語を入れ、音声を聞いて答えを確認しましょう。

1. Bob (　　　　) just (　　　　　) his homework.
2. Lisa (　　　　) (　　　　) (　　　　　) Japan.
3. Bob (　　　　) an (　　　　) (　　　　　) yesterday.
4. Ai (　　　　) (　　　　　) a couple of boys (　　　　　) the past five years.

# Practice 3  A-50  p. 98

日本語をヒントにしながら、それぞれの英文が答えとなるような英語での質問を書いてみましょう。そのあと音声を聞いて正解例を確認しましょう。

1. Yes. I went there, but it was closed. （図書館に昨日行ったか）

2. No. Is it a good movie? （『タイタニック』という映画を見たことがあるか）

3. Ah... maybe, I did. （自分の部屋の電気を消したか）

4. Oh, I've been just busy. （これまでどうしていたのか）

# Practice 4

例を参考にしながら自分のこれまでを振り返り、自分のための Personal History を完成させましょう。

例

**My Personal History**

| いつどこで生まれたか | I ( was born in Kobe in 2001 ). |
|---|---|
| 子供の頃は何になりたかったか | When I was a child, I ( wanted to be a taxi driver ). |
| 中学のときはどんなことをしていたか | I ( played baseball ) in junior high school. |
| 中学のとき以来、今もしていることは | I ( have been playing baseball since then ). |
| 高校のときはどんなことをしていたか | In high school, I ( practiced acting ). |
| 高校のとき以来、今もしていることは | I ( have been acting for more than three years ). |

**My Personal History**

| いつどこで生まれたか | I ( ). |
|---|---|
| 子供の頃は何になりたかったか | When I was a child, I ( ). |
| 中学のときはどんなことをしていたか | I ( ) in junior high school. |
| 中学のとき以来、今もしていることは | I ( ). |
| 高校のときはどんなことをしていたか | In high school, I ( ). |
| 高校のとき以来、今もしていることは | I ( ). |

# Practice 5

クラスメートと Practice 4 の答えをシェアしましょう。

---

▶ **Grammar in Action** ◀　Have you never...? の表現

「…したことがありますか」は Have you ever...? ですが、「…したことがありませんか」と問いかける場合は Have you never... ? という形を取ります。オリビア・ニュートン・ジョンの「そよ風の誘惑 ("Have You Never Been Mellow")」という歌のサビの部分では、次のような疑問文の歌詞が4つ出てきます。どんな意味か考えてみましょう。

Have you never been mellow?
Have you never tried to find a comfort from inside you?
Have you never been happy just to hear your song?
Have you never let someone else be strong?

# BASIC

## What are you going to do?

Unit 7

時制③：未来形

### Dialogue  A-52

青色部分に注意しながら会話を聞いてみましょう。

Lisa: What are you studying, Kaz? It's almost 11:00 p.m. The library will close very soon.
Kaz: I know. I'm writing a report for my economics class. And I'll also have a test next week.
Lisa: Oh, good luck. By the way, what are you going to do during the winter break? The dorm is going to close during the break.
Kaz: Is it? I didn't know that. Then, I have to find a place to stay.
Lisa: Why don't you come to my house and spend the Christmas vacation with my family?
Kaz: Oh, are you sure? That sounds wonderful. Thank you very much.
Lisa: No problem. Oh, Kaz, did you hear that?
Kaz: What?
Lisa: They said, "The library is closing in a minute."

### Warm Up  A-53 ▶ 55

英文を聞いて、ダイアログの内容と一致する場合はTを、一致しない場合はFを○で囲みましょう。

1. T / F
2. T / F
3. T / F

Unit 7　What are you going to do?

## ▶Tips for Grammar◀　時制③

**未来形**

未来のことを表すには2つの方法があります。1つは《be going to ＋動詞の原形》、もう1つは《will ＋動詞の原形》です。

　I am going to buy a car.　私は車を買う予定だ。
　I will be twenty next year.　私は来年20歳になる。

**be going to と will の違い**

どちらもこれから起こることを表すという点では同じですが、be going to は前から予定に組んであって「…する予定だ」と述べるときに使います。一方、will は意思を述べようとするときや、その場で急にあることをしようという気になった場合などに使います。また話し手の意思とは関係なく、ある事態が自然に起こるような場合にも使います。

　I'm going to have an interview next Saturday.　私は来週の土曜日、面接を受ける予定です。
　I will do my best.　私は全力を尽くします。
　I'll get it.　私が出るわ。（玄関の呼び鈴が鳴った場合や、電話が鳴った場合などで）
　It will be sunny tomorrow.　明日は晴れるだろう。

⇒ 詳しくは **100** ページ参照

## Practice 1

日本語のヒントを参考にして、（　）に適切な語を入れましょう。

1. 「メールするよ」と言うときは？

　I (　　　　) (　　　　) you when I get there.

2. プロポーズの言葉は？

　(　　　　) (　　　　) marry me?

3. 予定を尋ねるときは？

　What (　　　　) (　　　　) (　　　　) to do tonight?

4. 電話が鳴って、「自分が出るよ」と言うときは？

　I (　　　　) (　　　　) it.

5. 「ミルクがない」と言われたので、「買ってくるよ」と応じるときは？

　I (　　　　) (　　　　) some.

# Practice 2  A-56                              Hint p. 100

下の英文はイラスト内に矢印で示した人物のセリフです。（　）に適切な語を入れ、音声を聞いて答えを確認しましょう。

1. It (　　　　) (　　　　) (　　　　　) rain this afternoon.
2. My grandmother (　　　　) (　　　　) (　　　　　) next year.
3. (　　　　) (　　　　　) for London tomorrow morning.
4. Hurry! The concert (　　　　) about (　　　　) start.

# Practice 3 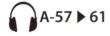 A-57 ▶ 61                         Hint p. 100

音声を聞いて（　）に適切な語を入れましょう。

1. (　　　　) (　　　　) (　　　　　) a call tonight.
2. (　　　　) (　　　　) (　　　　　) to attend the meeting next week?
3. He (　　　　) (　　　　) in Japan this evening.
4. (　　　　) (　　　　) (　　　　　) at 12:10.
5. He (　　　　) (　　　　) (　　　　　) an important lecture tonight.

Unit 7 What are you going to do?

# Practice 4

例を参考にしながら、この授業後の自分の予定を、be going to や will を使って下の枠内に書きましょう。

After this class, **I'm going to** have lunch with my friend at the school cafeteria.
In the afternoon, **I'll** have two more classes.
After school, **I'll probably** go to a gym and workout.
When I get home, **I'll** take a shower and eat dinner.
**I'm going to** study for the English test at night.

Your plan after this class:

# Practice 5

クラスメートと Practice 4 の答えをシェアしましょう。

---

▶ **Grammar in Action** ◀　未来を表す現在形進行形の用法

ユニバーサルスタジオのアトラクションでも有名になった映画『バック・トゥ・ザ・フューチャー』ですが、「未来へ帰る」というタイトルを奇異に感じたことはありませんか。1985年から1955年という過去へタイムスリップした主人公のマーティに対して、タイムマシンを発明したドクがこんなことを言いました。"Next Saturday night, we're sending you back to the future." つまり「過去から未来へ送り返す」という意味合いです。未来に向けて現時点で準備を進めているというときには、現在進行形の形で未来の意味合いを表すことができるので、このセリフの場合もイメージ的にそれに沿った用い方になっていると考えられます。

# BASIC

# Can I have a single room tonight?

## Unit 8

助動詞① : can / may

### Dialogue   A-63

青色部分に注意しながら会話を聞いてみましょう。

Ai: Hi. I don't have a reservation. Can I have a single room tonight?
Clerk: Let me check. Yes, we do have some single rooms available. Would you like a non-smoking room?
Ai: Yes. And if possible, can I have a room on a high floor?
Clerk: Yes, certainly. Which would you prefer, a room with a mountain view or a city view?
Ai: Well, can I have a room with a city view?
Clerk: Yes, you can. May I see your passport and credit card?
Ai: Here you are.
Clerk: Thank you very much.

### Warm Up   A-64 ▶ 66

英文を聞いて、ダイアログの内容と一致する場合はTを、一致しない場合はFを○で囲みましょう。

1. T / F
2. T / F
3. T / F

Unit 8　Can I have a single room tonight?

## ▶ Tips for Grammar ◀　can と be able to

### can の否定形
can の否定形は can't もしくは cannot と表記します。cannot は 1 語であることに注意しましょう。なお、can not という 2 語の形はあまり使うことがありません。過去形の場合は couldn't となります。

### can と be able to
「…できる」と言う場合、can の代わりに be able to を使うこともできます。未来の事柄を述べる場合は、will be able to（…できるだろう）となり、will can とは言わないので注意しましょう。

### could と was able to
「…する能力があった」と過去を振り返って言う場合は、could と was able to の両方を使うことができます。ただし、能力があって実際に実行したと言う場合は was able to を使い、could を用いることはできません。

　She could play tennis at four.　彼女は 4 歳でテニスができた。

　He was able to run 15 km yesterday.　彼は昨日、15 キロ走ることができた。

⇒ 詳しくは 102 ページ参照

# Practice 1

(　) の中から適切なほうを選び、完成した英文を日本語にしましょう。

1. I ( can / be able to ) eat very hot curry.

　　日本語：＿＿＿＿＿＿＿＿＿＿＿＿＿＿＿＿＿＿＿＿＿＿＿＿＿＿＿＿＿＿

2. You will ( can / be able to ) speak English soon.

　　日本語：＿＿＿＿＿＿＿＿＿＿＿＿＿＿＿＿＿＿＿＿＿＿＿＿＿＿＿＿＿＿

3. She ( can't / wasn't able to ) come to school yesterday.

　　日本語：＿＿＿＿＿＿＿＿＿＿＿＿＿＿＿＿＿＿＿＿＿＿＿＿＿＿＿＿＿＿

4. I ( can / cannot ) find my cell phone anywhere.

　　日本語：＿＿＿＿＿＿＿＿＿＿＿＿＿＿＿＿＿＿＿＿＿＿＿＿＿＿＿＿＿＿

5. He ( can't / couldn't ) come to the party tomorrow.

　　日本語：＿＿＿＿＿＿＿＿＿＿＿＿＿＿＿＿＿＿＿＿＿＿＿＿＿＿＿＿＿＿

# Practice 2  A-67　　　　　　　　Hint p. 102

下の英文はイラスト内に矢印で示した人物のセリフです。（　）に適切な語を入れ、音声を聞いて答えを確認しましょう。

1. You (　　　　) (　　　　) beer because you're too young.
2. (　　　　) (　　　　) (　　　　) me the salt?
3. (　　　　) (　　　　) (　　　　) the bathroom?
4. Amazing!  You (　　　　) (　　　　) five languages.

# Practice 3  A-68　　　　　　　　Hint p. 102

日本語をヒントにして（　）に適切な語を入れ、Aのセリフを完成させましょう。そのあと音声を聞いて答えを確認しましょう。

1. A: (　　　　) you (　　　　) (　　　　) with my homework?　宿題を手伝ってほしい

   B: I'm afraid I can't because I'm busy. Can you do it by yourself?

2. A: (　　　　) (　　　　) (　　　　) this credit card?　クレジットカードが使えるか

   B: Yes. Of course.

3. A: (　　　　) (　　　　) (　　　　) your name, please?　お名前は？

   B: My name is Anya.

4. A: (　　　　) (　　　　) (　　　　) some snow tonight.　今晩は雪かも

   B: Yeah, it's very cold outside.

# Practice 4

例を参考にしながら、下の表であなた自身の CAN-DO リストを完成させましょう。

例

When I was a child, I could run fast but I couldn't swim fast.
Now, I can write English well but I can't speak it fluently.
In the future, I think I'll be able to visit a lot of foreign countries but probably I won't be able to live in one of those countries permanently.

| could / couldn't |
| --- |
| When I was a child, I could (　　　　　　　) but I couldn't (　　　　　　　). |
| can / can't |
| Now, I can (　　　　　　　) but I can't (　　　　　　　). |
| will be able to / won't be able to |
| In the future, I think I'll be able to (　　　　　　　) but probably I won't be able to (　　　　　　　). |

# Practice 5

クラスメートと Practice 4 の答えをシェアしましょう。

---

▶ **Grammar in Action** ◀　　Can I...? と May I...? のニュアンスの違い

"Can I use your PC?" と尋ねるよりも、"May I use your PC?" のほうが丁寧な表現です。仲の良い友達同士なら Can I...? で構いませんが、初対面の人や目上の人などに対しては May I...? と尋ねるほうが無難です。また相手が "May I use your PC?" とあなたに尋ね、それを承諾する際に "Yes, you may." のように答えると無礼に聞こえます。そのときは "Yes, of course." や "Sure, go ahead." などと答えるとよいでしょう。

# BASIC

## That would be the perfect thing to do

Unit 9

助動詞② : could / would

### Dialogue  A-70

青色部分に注意しながら会話を聞いてみましょう。

Bob: It's cloudy outside. It could rain today.
Ai: Yes. The weather forecast says it's going to rain, so we can't go cycling.
Bob: No? Well, what would you like to do instead? Would you like to watch a video at home?
Ai: Ah, no, but I'd like to read a book.
Bob: Come on! Let's do something more fun. Something we can enjoy together.
Ai: I know. How about making some sweets? My mother and I would often bake cakes on a rainy day when I was a child.
Bob: That sounds great. That would be the perfect thing to do right now.

### Warm Up  A-71 ▶ 73

英文を聞いて、ダイアログの内容と一致する場合はTを、一致しない場合はFを○で囲みましょう。

1. T / F
2. T / F
3. T / F

Unit 9　That would be the perfect thing to do

## ▶ Tips for Grammar ◀　could と would

**could と would を使った丁寧な依頼**

Can you...? は「…してくれませんか」という意味ですが、can を could に換えて Could you...? にすると「…していただけませんか」という丁寧な表現になります。could の代わりに would を使って Would you...? にするとか、Could you possibly...? などの言い方をするとより丁寧な依頼の表現となります。また「…したい」というときに、I want to でなく I would like to を使うと丁寧な表現になります。丁寧な言い方として could と would を用いた場合には、そのいずれの語も過去の意味合いを含みません。

　Could you lend me some money?　お金を少し貸していただけませんか。
　Would you help me with my report?　レポートを手伝っていただけませんか。
　Would it be possible for you to send this letter to Japan?　この手紙を日本へ送っていただくことはできますか。

⇒ 詳しくは 104 ページ参照

## Practice 1

次の英文を丁寧な依頼の文にするにはどうすればよいでしょうか。could や would を使って書き換えましょう。

1. Give me a hand because I'm so busy.

2. Pass me the salt.

3. Send me an e-mail when you get there.

4. I want to go shopping this afternoon.

5. Do you want to join us for dinner?

6. What do you want to do tonight?

## Practice 2  A-74  Hint p. 104

下の英文はイラスト内に矢印で示した人物のセリフです。（ ）に適切な語を入れ、音声を聞いて答えを確認しましょう。

1. (            ) (            ) (            ) some dessert?
2. (            ) (            ) (            ) off the light when you leave?
3. (            ) (            ) (            ) me how to get to the library?
4. (            ) (            ) (            ) like to do on your holiday?

## Practice 3 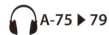 A-75 ▶ 79  Hint p. 104

音声を聞いて（ ）に適切な語を入れましょう。そのあと各英文の中で使われている would の意味合いとして最も適切なものを枠内から選び、[ ] に記号を入れましょう。

| a. 推量　　b. 過去の拒絶　　c. 過去の習慣　　d. 依頼　　e. 要望 |
|---|

1. Would (            ) (            ) the (            )? It's (            ) (            ) in here. [      ]
2. (            ) would (            ) the (            ) (            ). [      ]
3. I would (            ) (            ) (            ) this (            ) to Japan. [      ]
4. I would (            ) (            ) chess when (            ) (            ) in (            ). [      ]
5. She wouldn't (            ) second-hand (            ). [      ]

Unit 9　That would be the perfect thing to do

# Practice 4

日本国内で訪れたい都市を1つ選び、下の例を参考にしながら、次の①〜④について I'd like to の表現を用いた文を完成させましょう。

① 都市の名前
② 交通手段
③ 訪れたい時期
④ そこでやりたいこと2つ

I'd like to visit Sapporo in February.
I'd like to go there by airplane.
I'd like to go to the Sapporo Snow Festival and try Sapporo ramen.

| I'd like to visit ( ) in ( ). |
| I'd like to go there ( ). |
| I'd like to ( ) |
| and ( ). |

# Practice 5

クラスメートと Practice 4 の答えをシェアしましょう。

▶ Grammar in Action ◀　過去の習慣を表す would

would は丁寧な表現としてよく使われますが、過去によくやっていたことを思い出して言う場合にもよく用いられます。皆さんも一度は耳にしたことがあると思いますが、カーペンターズの "Yesterday Once More" という曲の出だしの歌詞は有名ですね。
"When I was young I'd listen to the radio, waiting for my favorite songs. When they played, I'd sing along, it made me smile."
この歌詞の中では、過去の習慣を表す would が効果的に使われています。

# BASIC

## Unit 10: Do I have to sign up for the lesson?

助動詞③：should / must / have to / had better

### Dialogue  A-81

青色部分に注意しながら会話を聞いてみましょう。

Kaz: Excuse me. I'm an exchange student from Japan. Is this the International Lounge?

Staff: Yes. You can learn a lot about foreign cultures and languages here.

Kaz: Could you tell me the rules of this lounge? Maybe there is something I should and shouldn't do.

Staff: Sure. We have three basic rules. You cannot smoke, of course. And you have to turn off your cell phone. More importantly, you must speak English as much as you can.

Kaz: I see. Is it OK to eat and drink here?

Staff: No problem.

Kaz: Do I have to sign up for the evening English lesson?

Staff: No, you don't have to, but you'd better come early.

### Warm Up  A-82 ▶ 84

英文を聞いて、ダイアログの内容と一致する場合はTを、一致しない場合はFを○で囲みましょう。

1. T / F
2. T / F
3. T / F

Unit 10　Do I have to sign up for the lesson?

## ▶Tips for Grammar◀　　must と have to

### must の用法

must は「…しなければならない」という義務を表し、話し手が主観的に義務や必要性を感じた場合に使います。「…してはいけない」という否定表現の場合は mustn't となります。

　You must pay at the entrance.　あなたは入口で料金を払わねばならない。
　You mustn't complain.　不満を言ってはいけません。

### have to の用法

have to は must と意味は同じですが、周囲の状況から客観的に判断して「…しなければならない」と感じられたときなどによく使われます。否定形は don't have to となり、「…しなくてもよい」という意味になります。

　I have to go to the hospital today.　私は今日、病院に行かないといけない。
　I don't have to work overtime today.　私は今日は残業しなくてもよい。

### 未来と過去を表す場合

must を使って未来や過去のことを表すことはできないので、そうした場合は have to を使うことになります。未来の場合には will have to、過去の場合には had to となります。

　I'll have to attend the meeting tomorrow.　私は明日、会議に出席しないといけないだろう。
　I won't have to attend the meeting tomorrow.　私は明日、会議に出席しなくてもよい。
　I had to attend the meeting yesterday.　私は昨日、会議に出席しないといけなかった。
　I didn't have to attend the meeting yesterday.　私は昨日、会議に出席しなくてもよかった。

⇒ 詳しくは 106 ページ参照

# Practice 1

日本語をヒントにして、（　）に適切な語を入れましょう。

1. You (　　　　) (　　　　　　) (　　　　　　　) quiet in the library.
　静かにしなくてはいけない

2. I (　　　　) (　　　　　　) to her.
　謝らなければならない

3. You (　　　　) (　　　　　　) (　　　　　　) by yourself.
　料理をしなければいけなかった

4. You (　　　　) (　　　　　　) the office rules.
　規則を破ってはならない

5. You (　　　　) (　　　　　) (　　　　　　) (　　　　　　　) off your phone in this area.
　電源を切る必要はない

45

# Practice 2  A-85 Hint p. 106

下の英文はイラスト内に矢印で示した人物のセリフです。（ ）に適切な語を入れ、音声を聞いて答えを確認しましょう。

1. (　　　　) (　　　　　　) follow the campus rules.
2. You (　　　　) (　　　　) (　　　　　) your umbrella.
3. You (　　　　) (　　　　) harder for the test tomorrow.
4. You (　　　　) have (　　　　) wash the dishes.

# Practice 3  A-86 Hint p. 106

（ ）の中から適切なほうを選び、音声を聞いて答えを確認しましょう。

1. You ( don't have to / mustn't ) pay for it. The lunch is on me.
2. You ( had not better / had better not ) bring a lot of cash to the party.
3. I will ( must / have to ) attend the meeting this afternoon.
4. Because of the rain, I didn't ( must / have to ) go hiking.
5. She is on a diet, so she ( must / mustn't ) be hungry.

# Practice 4

下の例を参考にしながら、表の中のフレーズを使って自分の家のルールを述べる英文を書き入れ、それを使って枠内の文章を完成させましょう。

**Rules in My House**

In my house, I...

| have to | |
| don't have to | |
| should / ought to | |
| had better | |

In my house, I have to ( wash dishes after dinner every day ) but I don't have to ( cook ). I also have to ( clean up the bathroom three times a week ). I should ( go grocery shopping for my mother ) but I seldom do it. I'd better ( clean up my room more often because it's so messy ).

**Rules in My House**

In my house, I have to (                                                          ) but I don't
have to (                              ). I also have to (                                   ).
I should (                                                                                   ).
I'd better (                                                                                 ).

# Practice 5

クラスメートと Practice 4 の答えをシェアしましょう。

---

▶ **Grammar in Action** ◀    mustn't の発音

must の否定表現 must not の省略形である mustn't を発音する場合は注意が必要です。発音記号で表すと [mʌ́snt] となり最初の t は発音しません。t の音を入れて発音すると、とてもぎこちなくなるはずです。fasten の場合に t を発音しないのと同じですね。

# BASIC

# I got fascinated with the beauty of the town

**Unit 11**

受動態

## Dialogue  B-02

青色部分に注意しながら会話を聞いてみましょう。

Kaz: I hear that you went to Amsterdam. How was your trip?

Lisa: Oh, it was fantastic! I got fascinated with the beauty of the town. This postcard is a souvenir for you.

Kaz: Thank you. It's Van Gogh's picture, isn't it?

Lisa: Yes. I went to the Van Gogh Museum. I saw a lot of pictures painted by him.

Kaz: Great! Where else did you go?

Lisa: Do you know *Anne's Diary*? It was written by Anne Frank. I went to the Anne Frank House, too. It was used by Anne's family for two years as a hiding house during World War II. I was really shocked at how scary their life was.

## Warm Up  B-03 ▶ 05

英文を聞いて、ダイアログの内容と一致する場合はTを、一致しない場合はFを○で囲みましょう。

1. T / F
2. T / F
3. T / F

Unit 11  I got fascinated with the beauty of the town

## ▶ Tips for Grammar ◀　受動態

受動態は「…が〜される」という意味を表し、《(助動詞＋) be 動詞＋動詞の過去分詞》の形をとります。

### 時制の表し方
受動態の文の時制は be 動詞で決まります。

　This bag is made in Italy.　このかばんはイタリア製だ。

　This temple was built in the 16th century.　この寺は 16 世紀に建てられた。

　A new French restaurant will be opened tomorrow.　新しいフランス料理店が明日オープンする。

### 受動態に〈by...〉を用いる場合
「誰［何］によって」を明確にする場合は、〈by...〉で表します。

　Our city was damaged by typhoon No.9.　私たちの街は台風 9 号によって被害を受けた。

### 受動態の疑問文と否定文
基本パターンは次のとおりです。

　Was the criminal arrested?　犯人は逮捕されたの？

　Who was invited to the party?　誰がパーティーに招待されたの？

　When will the news be announced?　いつそのニュースは発表されるの？

　The sports day was not postponed, although it rained.　雨だったが運動会は延期されなかった。

　The construction will not be completed by Friday.　工事は金曜日までには終わらないだろう。

⇒ 詳しくは 108 ページ参照

# Practice 1

(   ) の中の指示に従って、英文を書き換えましょう。

1. Our conversation was recorded.（否定文に）

2. My brother painted this wall.（受動態の文に）

3. She was invited to Kei's birthday party.（疑問文に）

4. Tokyo Tower was built in the 1950's.（下線部を問う疑問文に）

5. The new hotel was opened last week.（last week を next month に変えて未来を表す文に）

6. The president interviewed the three students.（受動態の文に）

# Practice 2  B-06    Hint p. 108

下の英文はイラストを描写しています。（ ）に適切な語を入れ、音声を聞いて答えを確認しましょう。

1. Their next concert will (　　　) (　　　) in New York.

2. The (　　　) is now (　　　) (　　　).

3. Flight 881 has (　　　) (　　　).

4. Yesterday's (　　　) time was (　　　) from 10:00 to 11:00.

# Practice 3  B-07    Hint p. 108

次の英文には間違いが1つあります。日本語をヒントにし、間違いの部分に下線を引いて訂正しましょう。そのあと音声を聞いて答えを確認しましょう。

1. I'm excited to the winter holiday.　　　　　　　　　…にわくわくしている

2. He was very disappointing with his test score.　　　…にがっかりした

3. This famous picture was painted from Picasso.　　　…によって描かれた

4. The concert hall filled with young women.　　　　　…で一杯だった

5. Haruki Murakami's works must known to the world.　…に知られている

# Practice 4

例を参考にしながら、自分の幼少時代について述べる枠内の英文を完成させましょう。

I was born in ( Kobe ) in ( 2000 ).
2000 年に神戸で生まれました。

I was raised in ( Osaka and Tokyo ).
大阪と東京で育ちました。

I was influenced most by ( my uncle ) when I was little.
小さいときに私が最も影響を受けたのは叔父です。

I was taken to the ( park near my house ) by ( my uncle ) very often.
家の近くの公園に叔父によく連れて行ってもらいました。

The happiest memory of my childhood is ( going to a zoo with him ).
子供時代の一番楽しかった思い出は、叔父と動物園に行ったことです。

> I was born in (　　　) in (　　　).
> I was raised in (　　　).
> I was influenced most by (　　　) when I was little.
> I was taken to the (　　　) by (　　　) very often.
> The happiest memory of my childhood is (　　　).

# Practice 5

クラスメートと Practice 4 の答えをシェアしましょう。

---

▶ **Grammar in Action** ◀　get を使った受動態

大ヒットしたディズニーの映画『アナと雪の女王』の英語の原題を知っていますか？ *Frozen* です。*frozen* は *freeze* の過去分詞で「凍った」という意味ですが、物についてだけではなく心についても使うことができます。映画を見るとわかりますが、あることがきっかけで心を閉ざしてしまったエルサ。そんな状態を Her heart got frozen.（彼女の心は凍りついてしまった）と表現することができます。こうした《get+ 過去分詞》も受動態の表現の一つです。

## BASIC

# Did you bring anything to eat?

**Unit 12**

不定詞①：基本用法

### Dialogue  B-09

青色部分に注意しながら会話を聞いてみましょう。

Lisa: We finally got to the top of the hill.
Kaz: Yes, we did it! I chose this place to see the beautiful ocean.
Lisa: Oh, it's so beautiful. I love it.
Kaz: I want you to enjoy the scenery and... special lunch!
Lisa: Did you bring anything to eat?
Kaz: Of course. Look at this.
Lisa: Wow! It's so sweet of you to make sandwiches for both of us.
Kaz: Sure. I'm happy to see your big smile.

### Warm Up  B-10 ▶ 12

英文を聞いて、ダイアログの内容と一致する場合は T を、一致しない場合は F を○で囲みましょう。

1. T / F
2. T / F
3. T / F

Unit 12　Did you bring anything to eat?

## ▶ Tips for Grammar ◀　to 不定詞

to 不定詞とは動詞の前に to を置き、《to ＋動詞の原形》の形で表したものです。その用法は以下の 3 つに大きく分かれます。

**名詞的用法**

名詞の働きをする to 不定詞で、「…すること」という意味を表します。

　　My dream is to be a dancer.　私の夢はダンサーになることだ。
　　It's easy to make friends.　友達を作ることは簡単だ。

**形容詞的用法**

名詞に意味を追加する to 不定詞で、名詞の後ろに置きます。「…するための〜」「…すべき〜」という意味を表します。

　　I have some things to do.　私にはしなくてはならないことがいくつかある。
　　I have good friends to consult with.　私には相談できる良い友達がいる。

**副詞的用法**

文や語句に意味を追加する to 不定詞で、「…するために」「…した結果〜」「…なので」という意味を表します。

　　I went to Kyoto to see my best friend.　私は親友に会うために京都に行った。
　　She grew up to be a photographer.　彼女は成長して写真家になった。
　　I was so glad to see you again.　私はあなたにまた会えてとても嬉しかった。

⇒ 詳しくは 110 ページ参照

## Practice 1

日本語に合うように（　）に適切な語を入れましょう。

1. 何か食べるものはある？
   Do you have (　　　　) (　　　　) (　　　　)?

2. 私は英語を勉強するために図書館に行った。
   I went to the library (　　　　) (　　　　) (　　　　).

3. 僕の夢はプロゴルファーになることだ。
   My dream (　　　　) (　　　　) (　　　　) a professional (　　　　).

4. 君の友達と話せてとても楽しかったよ。
   It was a lot of fun (　　　　) (　　　　) (　　　　) your friends.

## Practice 2  B-13  p. 110

下の英文はイラストを描写しています。（　）に適切な語を入れ、音声を聞いて答えを確認しましょう。

1. Kaz has a lot of homework (　　　　) (　　　　).
2. Ai (　　　　) every day (　　　　) lose weight.
3. One of Lisa's dreams is (　　　　) (　　　　) the aurora in Canada.
4. They are so (　　　　) (　　　　) (　　　　) each other again.

## Practice 3  B-14  p. 110

（　）内の語を並べ替えて正しい英文を作りましょう。ただし使わない語が1語入っています。また、文頭にくる語も小文字にしてあります。最後に音声を聞いて答えを確認しましょう。

1. ( exciting / is / it / new / places / to / visit / visiting ).

2. ( about / anything / are / do / have / talk / to / you )?

3. ( again / be / class / didn't / for / I / late / not / promised / to ).

4. ( beach / found / I / interesting / it / play / playing / to / volleyball ).

5. ( cook / dinner / for / it's / nice / of / to / you ).

# Practice 4

例を参考にしながら to 不定詞を使い、自分がどのような目的で物事に取り組んでいるかを述べる枠内の文を完成させましょう。

例

I entered the university to ( study tourism ).
観光を学ぶために大学に入りました。

I'm studying English to ( work at a travel agency after I graduate ).
卒業後旅行会社に勤めるために英語を勉強しています。

I'm working part-time and saving money to ( travel in Europe ).
ヨーロッパを旅行するためにアルバイトをしてお金を貯めています。

I'm practicing ( singing to become a professional singer in the future ).
将来プロの歌手になるために歌を練習しています。

I'd like to ( live by myself to be independent of my parents ).
親から自立するために一人暮らしをしたいです。

| | |
|---|---|
| I entered the university to ( | ). |
| I'm studying English to ( | ). |
| I'm working part-time and saving money to ( | ). |
| I'm practicing ( ) to ( | ). |
| I'd like to ( ) to ( | ). |

# Practice 5

クラスメートと Practice 4 の答えをシェアしましょう。

▶ Grammar in Action ◀　to 不定詞が用いられている名言

人生に役立つ名言の中でも to 不定詞は頻繁に使われています。例えば、"The best way to get something done is to begin." (何かをやり遂げるための最高の方法はまず始めることだ) というフレーズがあります。最初の不定詞句 to get something done は「…するための」を表す形容詞的用法として、2つ目の不定詞 to begin は「…すること」を表す名詞的用法として使われています。

# BASIC

## It's the most popular restaurant

Unit 13

比較

### Dialogue  B-16

青色部分に注意しながら会話を聞いてみましょう。

Bob: Wow! Isn't your box lunch great? It looks more delicious than my sandwiches.
Ai: I learned cooking from my big brother. He can cook much better than my mother.
Bob: Really? Why does he cook so well?
Ai: Well, he is a chef. He owns a little Japanese restaurant. It's one of the most popular restaurants in Kyoto.
Bob: Oh, that's amazing! Do you go there very often?
Ai: Sometimes, but not in spring because it's the busiest season.
Bob: I'd love to go to his restaurant when I visit Japan.
Ai: Then, you should come to Japan in a less busy season.

### Warm Up  B-17 ▶ 19

英文を聞いて、ダイアログの内容と一致する場合はTを、一致しない場合はFを○で囲みましょう。

1. T / F
2. T / F
3. T / F

Unit 13　It's the most popular restaurant

## ▶ Tips for Grammar ◀　比較

形容詞や副詞を使って比較表現の文を作る場合、以下の3つの形を使うことができます。

### 原級
《A ... as ＋形容詞／副詞の原級＋ as B》の形で「AはBと同じくらい〜」を表します。

My dog is as cute as his dog.　私の犬は彼の犬と同じくらいかわいい。

Ken can speak English as well as me.　ケンは僕と同じくらい英語を上手に話せる。

### 比較級
原則として《A ... 形容詞／副詞の比較級＋ than B》の形で「AはBより〜」を表します。

My dog is cuter than his dog.　私の犬は彼の犬よりかわいい。

Ken can speak English better than me.　ケンは僕より上手に英語を話せる。

Question 1 is more difficult than Question 2.　問題1は問題2より難しい。

### 最上級
《形容詞／副詞の最上級＋ in/of/among ...》の形で「…の中で最も〜」を表します。

My dog is the cutest in the world.　私の犬は世界で一番かわいい。

Ken can speak English best among his friends.　ケンは友達の中で一番上手に英語を話せる。

Question 1 is the most difficult of the five.　問題1は5つの問題の中で最も難しい。

通常、比較級は原級に -er をつけて、最上級は原級に -est をつけて表しますが、2音節の語の大半と3音節以上の語の場合は原級の前に more や most を置いて表します。

⇒ 詳しくは **112** ページ参照

## Practice 1

日本語に合うように（　）に適切な語を入れましょう。

1. 私は母と同じくらいの身長だ。
   I'm (　　　　) (　　　　) (　　　　) my mother.

2. 僕のスマートフォンは彼のほど新しくない。
   My smartphone is not (　　　　) (　　　　) (　　　　) his.

3. 彼女のアパートは私のアパートより狭い。
   Her apartment is (　　　　) (　　　　) my apartment.

4. Q2 より Q1 のほうが簡単に答えられる。
   You can (　　　　) Q1 (　　　　) (　　　　) (　　　　) Q2.

5. シーフードピザがこのレストランで一番おいしい料理だ。
   The seafood pizza is (　　　　) (　　　　) (　　　　) dish in this restaurant.

# Practice 2 🎧 B-20  Hint p. 112

下の英文はイラストを描写しています。（ ）に適切な語を入れ、音声を聞いて答えを確認しましょう。

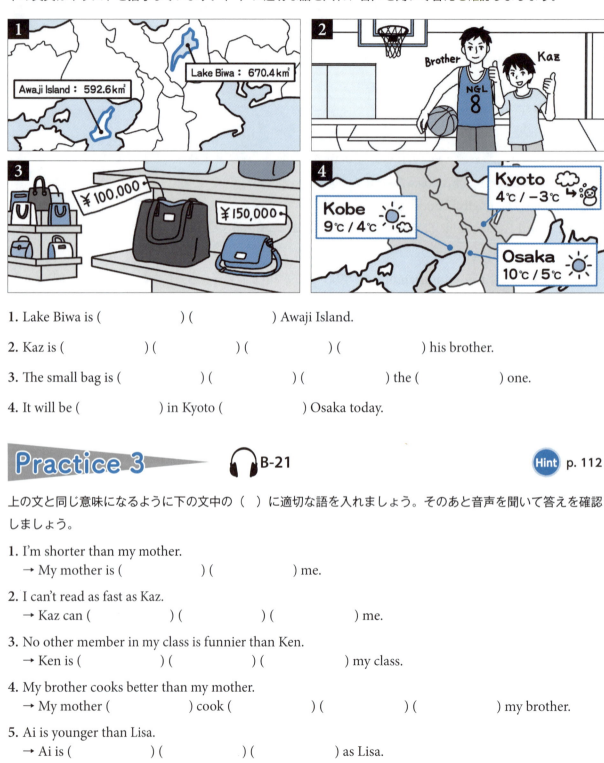

1. Lake Biwa is (　　　) (　　　　) Awaji Island.

2. Kaz is (　　　) (　　　) (　　　　) (　　　　) his brother.

3. The small bag is (　　　　) (　　　　) (　　　　) the (　　　　) one.

4. It will be (　　　　) in Kyoto (　　　　) Osaka today.

# Practice 3 🎧 B-21  Hint p. 112

上の文と同じ意味になるように下の文中の（ ）に適切な語を入れましょう。そのあと音声を聞いて答えを確認しましょう。

1. I'm shorter than my mother.
   → My mother is (　　　　) (　　　　) me.

2. I can't read as fast as Kaz.
   → Kaz can (　　　　) (　　　　) (　　　　) me.

3. No other member in my class is funnier than Ken.
   → Ken is (　　　　) (　　　　) (　　　　) my class.

4. My brother cooks better than my mother.
   → My mother (　　　　) cook (　　　　) (　　　　) (　　　　) my brother.

5. Ai is younger than Lisa.
   → Ai is (　　　　) (　　　　) (　　　　) as Lisa.

Unit 13　It's the most popular restaurant

# Practice 4

例を参考にしながら、比較（原級・比較級・最上級）の表現を使って好きなアーティストグループを紹介する文を枠内に書いてみましょう。

**例　One of My Favorite Singing Groups**　 B-22

One of my favorite singing groups is <u>Arashi</u>.
They are ( one of the most popular ) groups in (Japan).
There are ( five ) members.
<u>Ono</u> is the ( oldest ) in the group.
<u>Aiba</u> is as ( old ) as <u>Sakurai</u>.
<u>Matsumoto</u> is ( taller ) than <u>Ninomiya</u>.
I like <u>Sakurai</u> best because I think he is the ( most handsome ).
In my opinion, <u>Ono</u> can sing best and <u>Matsumoto</u> is the ( funniest ).

**One of My Favorite Singing Groups**

One of my favorite singing groups is _____.
They are ( _____ ) groups in ( _____ ).
There are ( _____ ) members.
_____ is the ( _____ ) in the group.
_____ is as ( _____ ) as _____.
_____ is ( _____ ) than _____.
I like _____ best because I think he/she is the ( _____ ).
In my opinion, _____ can sing best and _____ is the ( _____ ).

# Practice 5

クラスメートと **Practice 4** の答えをシェアしましょう。

---

▶ **Grammar in Action** ◀　比較級を用いた文での than の省略

比較級を用いる場合、会話では than を省略することがよくあります。以下はその好例です。
I'll try harder.（もっとがんばるよ）　Can you stay longer?（もう少しいられる？）
Let's talk more.（もっと話そうよ）　Couldn't be better!（最高！）
I can't love you more.（この上なく愛しているよ）

# BASIC

# The guy who moved next door is very strange

**Unit 14**

関係詞①：関係代名詞

## Dialogue  B-23

青色部分に注意しながら会話を聞いてみましょう。

Ai: The guy who moved next door is really very strange.
Bob: Really? In what way?
Ai: He is always wearing gold jewelry that looks very heavy and expensive. At night, he sometimes makes strange noises!
Bob: I see. Is there anything else that bothers you?
Ai: The other day, he had a visitor whose face was covered with a big mask!
Bob: Are they gangsters or something?
Ai: I don't know. Anyway, I want to move out. I can't stand it anymore.
Bob: You should start looking for an apartment which is much closer to the university.

## Warm Up 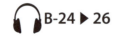 B-24 ▶ 26

英文を聞いて、ダイアログの内容と一致する場合はTを、一致しない場合はFを○で囲みましょう。

1. T / F
2. T / F
3. T / F

60

Unit 14　The guy who moved next door is very strange

## ▶Tips for Grammar◀　関係代名詞

**関係代名詞の用法**

2つの文を1つに結びつける代名詞のことを関係代名詞と呼びます。また、関係代名詞の前に置かれる名詞のことを先行詞と呼びます。

| 先行詞 | 主格（…は） | 所有格（…の） | 目的格（…を、に）※省略可 |
|---|---|---|---|
| 人 | who / that | whose | who(m) / that |
| 人以外 | which / that |  | which / that |

※ that は人が先行詞の場合よりも、人以外が先行詞の場合によく使われます。

I have a friend who lives in Paris.　私にはパリに住んでいる友達がいる。
I don't like movies which / that have sad endings.　私は悲しい結末の映画は好きではない。
I saw a strange person whose hair was green.　髪の毛が緑色の変わった人を見た。
The professor ( who(m) / that ) I wanted to see was not in her office.　私が会いたかった教授はオフィスにいなかった。
The dress ( which / that ) I bought yesterday was on sale.　私が昨日買ったドレスはセール価格だった。

⇒ 詳しくは114ページ参照

## Practice 1

（　）に適切な関係代名詞を入れましょう。ただし、that 以外の関係代名詞を使ってみましょう。

1. In my class, there are several people (　　　　) can speak Chinese very well.
2. This is the man (　　　　) I saw in the convenience store yesterday.
3. Do you have a friend (　　　　) has been to Egypt?
4. I know someone (　　　　) sister is a Hollywood star.
5. The pancakes (　　　　) I ate yesterday were very delicious.
6. Can you see the girl (　　　　) dress is very similar to mine?

# Practice 2  B-27  p. 114

下の英文はイラスト内に矢印で示した人物のセリフです。（ ）に適切な語を入れ、音声を聞いて答えを確認しましょう。

1. Look at the dog (　　　　) is (　　　　) a banana!
2. Where are the (　　　　)(　　　　)(　　　　) in the refrigerator?
3. The actor (　　　　) role is the police officer (　　　　) one of my old friends.
4. Do you know the man (　　　　)(　　　　)(　　　　) on the stage?

# Practice 3  B-28  p. 114

下線部の語を先行詞にして that 以外の関係代名詞を使い、2 つの文を 1 つにまとめましょう。そのあと音声を聞いて答えを確認しましょう。

1. I have a <u>cousin</u>. He lives in Honolulu.
   →
2. The action <u>movie</u> was boring. I watched it last night.
   →
3. Mr. Miyazaki is a great movie <u>director</u>. His works are popular in the world.
   →
4. The <u>girl</u> was my best friend. Mike fell in love with her.
   →
5. Jim is working for a <u>company</u>. It makes copy machines.
   →

# Practice 4

例を参考にしながら、自分自身のことについて述べる枠内の英文を完成させましょう。

例

The person whom I can trust most is ( my father ).
( Hiromi ) is my best friend who ( can understand and help me ).
The person who usually cooks for me is ( my grandmother ).
The TV program which makes me laugh most is ( "Odoru! Samma Goten!!" ).
The song that cheers me up most is ( "Makenaide" ).
I have a friend whose ( cousin is a popular model ).

> The person whom I can trust most is (　　　　　　).
> (　　　　　) is my best friend who (　　　　　　　　　　　　　　　　).
> The person who usually cooks for me is (　　　　　　　　).
> The TV program which makes me laugh most is (　　　　　　　　　　).
> The song that cheers me up most is (　　　　　　　　　).
> I have a friend whose (　　　　　　　　　　　　　　).

# Practice 5

クラスメートと Practice 4 の答えをシェアしましょう。

---

▶ **Grammar in Action** ◀　　文学作品で多用される関係代名詞

関係代名詞はおとぎ話の序盤で使われることがよくあります。
　"Once upon a time, there was a beautiful young girl whose stepmother always made her stay home with the baby."「昔むかし、継母にいつも家で子守をするよう押し付けられた美しい娘がいました」(『ラビリンス／魔王の迷宮』より)
また、関係代名詞は本のタイトルの中でも使われることがあります。例えば『金の卵を産むニワトリ』というイソップ童話の英語のタイトルは *The Goose That Laid the Golden Egg* です。

# BASIC

## If you were me, where would you go?

**Unit 15**

仮定法①：仮定法過去

### Dialogue 🎧 B-30

青色部分に注意しながら会話を聞いてみましょう。

Lisa: You know what? You won't believe this.
Kaz: What is it?
Lisa: I applied for a photo contest and won the first prize. I got a free airline ticket for overseas travel.
Kaz: Really? Congratulations! You are amazing.
Lisa: Thank you. I don't know where to go. If you were me, where would you go?
Kaz: If I were you, I would go to Canada and see Niagara Falls.
Lisa: That sounds nice. Oh, I just remembered a place I've wanted to visit. Machu Picchu in Peru!
Kaz: That would be very interesting, too.

### Warm Up 🎧 B-31 ▶ 33

英文を聞いて、ダイアログの内容と一致する場合はTを、一致しない場合はFを○で囲みましょう。

1. T / F
2. T / F
3. T / F

Unit 15　If you were me, where would you go?

## ▶ Tips for Grammar ◀　仮定法過去

現在のことに関して、事実ではないことや実現の可能性がないことを述べるときに使われる表現が仮定法過去です。現在のことであっても過去形を用います。日本語でも「もし宝くじが当たったら、外国旅行をするのに。」と言うように、「当たった」という過去形を使いますね。これと同じです。

### 基本形
《If + 主語 + （助）動詞の過去形 , 主語 + would/could/might + 動詞の原形》「もし…ならば、〜なのに」

　　If I had a long vacation, I could go to Europe.　長い休みがあればヨーロッパに行けるのに。
　　If I were you, I would marry him.　私があなたなら、彼と結婚するわ。

### I wish を使った表現
《I wish + 主語 + （助）動詞の過去形》「…ならいいのに」「…できたらいいのに」

　　I wish I were a millionaire.　私が億万長者ならいいのに。
　　I wish I could play the piano.　私がピアノを弾けたらいいのに。

### if 節が省略された形

　　Your grandmother would be very happy to see you.　おばあちゃんは君に会えたならきっと喜ぶよ。

⇒ 詳しくは **116** ページ参照

# Practice 1

日本語訳に合うように（　）に適切な語を入れましょう。

1. 車を持っていれば、友達と伊豆にドライブに行けるのに。
   If I (　　　　　) a car, I (　　　　　　　) drive to Izu with my friends.

2. 100万円当たったら、あなたは何を買う？
   (　　　　　) you (　　　　　　) one million yen, what (　　　　　　) you (　　　　　　)?

3. もし今週末ひまなら、買い物に行くのに。
   (　　　　) (　　　　　　) were (　　　　　) this weekend, I (　　　　　) (　　　　　)
   (　　　　).

4. 自分が有名な歌手だったらいいのに。
   I (　　　　　) I (　　　　　) a famous singer.

5. 今晩あなたと映画を見に行けたらいいのに。
   I wish I (　　　　　) (　　　　　) to see the (　　　　　) with you this (　　　　　).

6. 自分が英語を流ちょうに話せたらいいのに。
   (　　　　) (　　　　　) (　　　　　) (　　　　　) (　　　　　) (　　　　　)
   fluently.

# Practice 2  Hint p. 116

下の英文はイラスト内に矢印で示した人物のセリフです。（　）に適切な語を入れ、音声を聞いて答えを確認しましょう。

1. If I were you, I (　　　　) go (　　　　　) the (　　　　).
2. If I were you, I (　　　　) (　　　　　) a (　　　　).
3. If I were you, I (　　　　) (　　　　　) (　　　　).
4. If I were you, I (　　　　) (　　　　　) it to (　　　　) (　　　　).

# Practice 3  Hint p. 116

音声を聞いて（　）に適切な語を入れましょう。

1. I (　　　　) I (　　　　) (　　　　).
2. I wish I (　　　　) (　　　　) (　　　　).
3. I wish I (　　　　) (　　　　) (　　　　).
4. I wish I (　　　　) (　　　　) (　　　　).
5. I wish I (　　　　) (　　　　　) all over the (　　　　).

# Practice 4

海外のどこの国にでも行ける航空券が 2 枚当たったら、あなたはどこに行きますか。下の例を参考にしながら、次の情報を枠内の空所に入れて英文を完成させましょう。

1. The person whom you would give one ticket to （一緒に行きたい人）
2. The place you would visit （訪れたい場所）
3. Three activities you would do （そこでやってみたいこと 3 つ）

例

If I won two airplane tickets, I would give one ticket to ( my best friend Hiromi ), and go to ( Hawaii ) together.
We would ( stay in a nice hotel in Waikiki and enjoy shopping ).
We would also ( climb Diamond Head to see a beautiful view from there ).
On the last day, we would ( eat delicious seafood in a restaurant on the beach ).

> If I won two airplane tickets, I would give one ticket to (　　　　　),
> and go to (　　　　　) together.
> We would (　　　　　).
> We would also (　　　　　).
> On the last day, we would (　　　　　).

# Practice 5

クラスメートと Practice 4 の答えをシェアしましょう。

---

▶ **Grammar in Action** ◀　**if 節が省略された仮定法過去**

映画『ハリー・ポッターと賢者の石』の中で、ダンブルドア校長が "The happiest man on Earth <u>would</u> look into the mirror and see only himself exactly as he is."「もし世界一の幸せ者がこの鏡を見たら、あるがままの自分が正確に映し出されるだろう」と言うシーンがあります。このセリフは if 節が省略された仮定法過去の表現です。

## PLUS

# My hobby is playing sports

**Unit 16**

動名詞

## Dialogue  🎧 B-41

青色部分に注意しながら会話を聞いてみましょう。

Lisa: Do you have any hobbies, Kaz?
Kaz: My hobby is playing sports. Especially, I love playing soccer.
Lisa: I see. I don't play any sports, but I enjoy watching soccer games.
Kaz: How about you? What's your hobby?
Lisa: I like walking in nature. Are you interested in hiking?
Kaz: Yes. Hiking is a lot of fun, isn't it? Say, why don't we do it together this weekend?
Lisa: Sounds great! Where to?
Kaz: Let me check with my smartphone. I'm good at getting the latest information.

## Warm Up  🎧 B-42 ▶ 44

英文を聞いて、ダイアログの内容と一致する場合はTを、一致しない場合はFを○で囲みましょう。

1. T / F
2. T / F
3. T / F

Unit 16　My hobby is playing sports

## ▶ Tips for Grammar ◀　動名詞

動名詞は［動詞 -ing］の形で名詞の働きを持ち、「…すること」という意味を表します。動名詞は繰り返し行っていることを表すときによく使われます。動名詞の主な用法は次のとおりです。

**主語**
　Studying English is very important.　英語を学ぶことはとても大切だ。

**補語**
　My hobby is playing tennis.　私の趣味はテニスをすることだ。

**目的語**
　I like watching movies.　私は映画を見るのが好きだ。

特に前置詞の後ろに動詞を続ける場合は動名詞（の形）になります。
　I'm interested in studying abroad.　私は留学に興味がある。
　Are you good at cooking?　あなたは料理が得意なの？
　Thank you for helping me with my homework.　宿題を手伝ってくれてありがとう。

⇒ 詳しくは118ページ参照

# Practice 1

日本語に合うように（　）に適切な語を入れましょう。

1. 私の趣味は音楽鑑賞だ。
　My hobby is (　　　　　) (　　　　　) (　　　　　).

2. 舞台の上で踊ることはとてもわくわくする。
　(　　　　　) on the stage is very (　　　　　).

3. 僕は野球をするのが大好きだ。
　I (　　　　　) (　　　　　) (　　　　　).

4. 彼女は悲しいニュースを見るのが好きではない。
　She doesn't (　　　　　) (　　　　　) sad news.

5. 私は中国語を学ぶことに興味がある。
　I'm (　　　　　) in (　　　　　) (　　　　　).

6. 君はスポーツをするのが得意かい？
　Are you (　　　　　) at (　　　　　) (　　　　　)?

# Practice 2

 B-45     Hint p. 118

下の英文はイラスト内に矢印で示した人物のセリフです。（ ）に適切な語を入れ、音声を聞いて答えを確認しましょう。

1. I like (　　　　) (　　　　) than (　　　　).
2. I want to go to Europe, but I'm (　　　　) of (　　　　).
3. Thank you (　　　　) (　　　　) my (　　　　).
4. I'm looking forward (　　　　) (　　　　) Italy.

# Practice 3

 B-46     Hint p. 118

英文には間違いが1つあります。日本語をヒントにし、間違いの部分に下線を引いて訂正しましょう。そのあと音声を聞いて答えを確認しましょう。

1. Saying not "Thank you" is sad. 　　　　「ありがとう」と言わないことは悲しいことだ。

2. I hate frequent lying. 　　　　君がよく嘘をつくことがいやだ。

3. I practice to play the guitar every day. 　　　　毎日ギターの練習をする。

4. Don't forget calling me at 3:00. 　　　　忘れずに3時に私に電話しなさい。

5. I'm used to wake up early. 　　　　早起きに慣れている。

Unit 16　My hobby is playing sports

# Practice 4

例を参考にしながら、動名詞を使って自分の興味や関心のあることを述べる枠内の文を完成させましょう。

( Practicing the violin ) is a lot of fun for me.
I enjoy ( reading comic books ) on weekends.
I'm good at ( drawing pictures ).
I'm interested in ( visiting a lot of national parks in Japan ).
I don't like ( going to crowded places on weekends ).
I'm used to ( cooking dinner for my family ).
I look forward to ( going to Australia this summer ).

| |
|---|
| (　　　　　　　　　　　　　　　　　　　　　) is a lot of fun for me. |
| I enjoy (　　　　　　　　　　　　　　　　　　　) on weekends. |
| I'm good at (　　　　　　　　　　　　　　　　　　　　　　). |
| I'm interested in (　　　　　　　　　　　　　　　　　　　). |
| I don't like (　　　　　　　　　　　　　　　　　　　　　　). |
| I'm used to (　　　　　　　　　　　　　　　　　　　　　　). |
| I look forward to (　　　　　　　　　　　　　　　　　　　). |

# Practice 5

クラスメートと Practice 4 の答えをシェアしましょう。

▶ **Grammar in Action** ◀ 　feel like *doing* を使って自分の気分を表そう

「…したい気分だ」という意味の feel like *doing* も動名詞を用いた表現で、会話の中でよく使われます。I feel like singing.（歌いたい気分だ）、I feel like having Italian for lunch.（ランチにはイタリアンを食べたい気分よ）、I don't feel like talking.（話したい気分じゃないんだけど）などと、I want to *do* の代わりに I feel like *doing* を使ってみると英会話表現の幅が広がります。

**PLUS**

# I'm too excited to sleep tonight

**Unit 17**

不定詞②：応用構文と原形不定詞

## Dialogue  🎧 B-48

青色部分に注意しながら会話を聞いてみましょう。

Ai: Our basketball club camp in Florida is coming up! I'm so happy that I can go to Florida with you!

Bob: Yeah. Maybe we can go to Disney World in our free time.

Ai: I think we'll be too busy to do that. Our coach will not let us go anyway.

Bob: I see. By the way, did you tell all of the club members to come to the airport at 10:00 a.m. tomorrow?

Ai: Yes. I'm too excited to sleep tonight.

Bob: Don't forget to pack everything you need. See you tomorrow, then.

## Warm Up  🎧 B-49 ▶ 51

英文を聞いて、ダイアログの内容と一致する場合は T を、一致しない場合は F を○で囲みましょう。

1. T / F
2. T / F
3. T / F

Unit 17　I'm too excited to sleep tonight

## ▶ Tips for Grammar ◀　to 不定詞と原形不定詞の用法

《動詞＋目的語＋ to 不定詞》
この表現における目的語は「人」である場合がほとんどです。

　　I asked her to buy some juice.　私は彼女にジュースを買ってくれるよう頼んだ。
　　My parents want me to be a doctor.　両親は私に医者になってほしいと思っている。
　　I got my brother to fix my watch.　私は兄に時計を直してもらった。

《動詞＋目的語＋原形不定詞》
原形不定詞をとる動詞は次の 2 種類で、この表現でも目的語は主に「人」です。

　使役動詞：have、let、make
　　I had my friend cut my hair.　私は友達に髪の毛を切ってもらった。
　　My father let me go driving at night.　父は私を夜ドライブに行かせてくれた。
　　He made me wait for two hours.　彼は私を 2 時間待たせた。

　知覚動詞：feel、hear、notice、see、watch など
　　I felt someone touch my hair.　誰かが私の髪を触るのを私は感じた。
　　I heard my boyfriend call my name.　ボーイフレンドが私の名前を呼ぶのが聞こえた。
　　I saw him open the gate.　彼が門を開けるのを私は見た。

⇒ 詳しくは 120 ページ参照

## Practice 1

日本語に合うように（　）の中に適切な語を入れましょう。

1. 私に電話をかけ直すよう彼女に言ってくれた？
　　Did you (　　　　　) her (　　　　　　) (　　　　　　　) me back?
2. 私は兄にお弁当を作ってもらった。
　　I (　　　　　) my big (　　　　　) (　　　　　　) a box lunch.
3. 彼が有名な歌手とデートするのを見た。
　　I (　　　　　) him (　　　　　) a (　　　　　) (　　　　　　).
4. 母はいつも私に皿洗いをさせるの。
　　My mother always (　　　　　　) me (　　　　　) the dishes.
5. あなたには成功してもらいたい。
　　I (　　　　　) you (　　　　　) (　　　　　) (　　　　　　).
6. 私は両親が引っ越しについて話すのを聞いた。
　　I (　　　　　) my parents (　　　　　) (　　　　　　) moving.

## Practice 2  B-52 　　　　　　　　　　　　　　Hint p. 120

下の英文はイラスト内に矢印で示した人物のセリフです。（ ）に適切な語を入れ、音声を聞いて答えを確認しましょう。

1. Please (　　　　) me (　　　　) (　　　　) (　　　　) math questions.
2. I wonder (　　　　) (　　　　) (　　　　) visit.
3. Could you (　　　　) me (　　　　) (　　　　) (　　　　) this machine?
4. Tell me (　　　　) (　　　　) (　　　　) when I go to Osaka.

## Practice 3  B-53 　　　　　　　　　　　　　　Hint p. 120

《too ... to 不定詞》もしくは《... enough to 不定詞》を使い、文を書き換えましょう。そのあと音声を聞いて答えを確認しましょう。

1. This dish is so spicy that I can't eat it.
　→
2. He is so busy that he can't take any days off.
　→
3. My friend was so kind that she helped me with my homework.
　→
4. This room is so big that 40 students can dance together.
　→

# Practice 4

例を参考にしながら、不定詞の表現を使いながら自分のことについての枠内の英文を完成させましょう。

例

I'm too ( shy ) to ( speak in front of people ).
I'm ( kind ) enough to ( help people in need ).
My parents make me ( eat vegetables every day ).
My family lets me ( live by myself ).
( My big brother ) taught me how to ride a bicycle.
I can teach you how to ( cook delicious beef bowl ).
To tell you the truth, I ( am working as a model ).

| |
|---|
| I'm too (　　　) to (　　　　　　　　　　　). |
| I'm (　　　　) enough to (　　　　　　　　　). |
| My parents make me (　　　　　　　　　　　). |
| My family lets me (　　　　　　　　　). |
| (　　　　　　　　　) taught me how to ride a bicycle. |
| I can teach you how to (　　　　　　　　　　　). |
| To tell you the truth, I (　　　　　　　　　　　). |

# Practice 5

クラスメートと Practice 4 の答えをシェアしましょう。

▶ **Grammar in Action** ◀　口語でよく使われる《疑問詞 + to 不定詞》

《疑問詞 + to 不定詞》は日常会話でよく使われる表現です。例えば、映画『ローマの休日』の最後の別れのシーンで、王女アンが "I don't know how to say good-bye." 「なんてさよならを言っていいのかわからないわ」と言います。また、同作品のリメーク版である『ノッティングヒルの恋人』では、主人公ウィリアムがアナの部屋を訪れたとき、意外なことにアナの恋人が待っていたという場面では、アナがウィリアムに "I'm sorry. I don't know what to say." 「ごめんなさい。なんて言ったらいいのかわからない」と言っています。

# I watched a very exciting movie

Unit 18

分詞

## Dialogue 🎧 B-55

青色部分に注意しながら会話を聞いてみましょう。

Bob: How was your weekend?
Ai: Not bad. Actually, it was a *relaxing* weekend. I watched a very *exciting* movie. It's an action film *named* Die Hard.
Bob: I also watched a DVD. Guess which movie I watched. It's one of the most famous *animated* movies *directed* by Hayao Miyazaki.
Ai: Isn't it *My Neighbor Totoro*?
Bob: Yeah, that's right. It's kind of old because it was released in 1988, but it's still very popular.
Ai: I love Totoro, too! Isn't Totoro very cute and *amusing*?

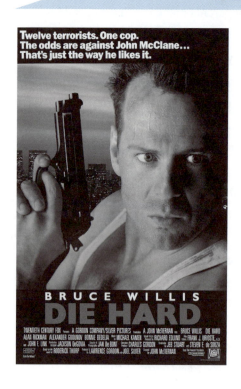

## Warm Up 🎧 B-56 ▶ 58

英文を聞いて、ダイアログの内容と一致する場合はTを、一致しない場合はFを○で囲みましょう。

1. T / F
2. T / F
3. T / F

# Unit 18　I watched a very exciting movie

## ▶Tips for Grammar◀　分詞

分詞には、現在分詞と過去分詞の2種類があります。

**現在分詞**

動詞に -ing が付いた形で「…する、…している」の意味を表し、次の用法があります。

① 後ろの名詞を修飾する

　I like relaxing music.　私はリラックスさせてくれる音楽が好きだ。

　There is boiling water in the pot.　鍋の中には沸騰しているお湯が入っている。

② 前の名詞を修飾する

　Look at the boy dancing on the platform!　プラットホームで踊っている少年を見て！

　Who is the woman playing the piano over there?　あそこでピアノを弾いている女性は誰？

③ 動詞の進行形として働く

　They are playing tennis now.　彼らは今テニスをしている。

　We were singing at that time.　そのとき私たちは歌っていた。

**過去分詞**

動詞に -ed などが付いた形や動詞が不規則に変化した形で「…された、…されている」の意味を表し、次の用法があります。

① 後ろの名詞を修飾する

　This is a hidden camera.　これは隠しカメラ（＝隠されたカメラ）だ。

　Do you often eat boiled eggs?　あなたはゆで卵（＝ゆでられた卵）をよく食べる？

② 前の名詞を修飾する

　This is the picture painted by Picasso.　これはピカソによって描かれた絵だ。

　The lunch cooked by mother was delicious.　母が作ってくれた昼食はおいしかった。

⇒詳しくは **122** ページ参照

## Practice 1

意味の通る文になるように、（　）の中の動詞を現在分詞または過去分詞に変えましょう。

1. Are you watching a baseball game on TV? Look at the ( excite ) audience!
2. What should I do with this ( break ) glass?
3. The ( steal ) wallet was found.
4. Did you see the beautiful ( rise ) sun this morning?
5. I saw a man ( walk ) with a monkey.
6. I bought a book ( write ) by Haruki Murakami.

# Practice 2  B-59　　　Hint p. 122

下の英文はイラスト内に矢印で示した人物のセリフです。（　）に適切な語を入れ、音声を聞いて答えを確認しましょう。

1. Look at that girl (　　　　　) the (　　　　　) there.
2. I heard the (　　　　　) news on the (　　　　　).
3. I don't like that (　　　　　) (　　　　　).
4. I watched the latest movie (　　　　　) (　　　　　) Steven Spielberg.

# Practice 3  B-60　　　Hint p. 122

日本語をヒントにして、（　）に適切な語を入れましょう。そのあと音声を聞いて答えを確認しましょう。

1. (　　　　) (　　　　), I don't like him.　　　　　　　　　　率直に言えば
2. (　　　　) (　　　　) this map, there is a station near here.　…によると
3. (　　　　) (　　　　) the sky, it will start raining soon.　　…から判断すると
4. (　　　　) (　　　　), she is a popular singer.　　　　　　　一般的に言えば
5. (　　　　) (　　　　) Akira, I haven't seen him for two years.　…と言えば

Unit 18　I watched a very exciting movie

# Practice 4

例を参考にしながら、分詞を使って自分の気持ちや感情を述べる枠内の文を完成させましょう。

例

( My cat ) is amusing to me.　　　　　　　　楽しませてくれるもの
( The marketing class ) is boring for me.　　退屈なこと
( Starting something new ) is exciting for me.　わくわくすること
I'm worried about ( my grades ).　　　　　心配なこと
I'm satisfied with ( my club activity ).　　満足していること
I'm terrified of ( dogs ).　　　　　　　　すごく怖いこと

(　　　　　　　　　　　　　　　　　　　　　　　　　　　) is amusing to me.
(　　　　　　　　　　　　　　　　　　　　　　　　　　　) is boring for me.
(　　　　　　　　　　　　　　　　　　　　　　　　　　　) is exciting for me.
I'm worried about (　　　　　　　　　　　　　　　　　　　　　　　　　).
I'm satisfied with (　　　　　　　　　　　　　　　　　　　　　　　　　).
I'm terrified of (　　　　　　　　　　　　　　　　　　　　　　　　　　).

# Practice 5

クラスメートと Practice 4 の答えをシェアしましょう。

▶ **Grammar in Action** ◀　　日本語化している食べ物の名前

《過去分詞＋名詞》の表現の中には、カタカナの日本語になって普段の生活でよく使われているものが結構あります。特に食べ物の名称に多く、以下はその一例です。

　　fried chicken（フライドチキン）　　　iced coffee（アイスコーヒー）
　　frozen yogurt（フローズンヨーグルト）　scrambled eggs（スクランブルエッグ）
　　smoked salmon（スモークサーモン）

カタカナで表された日本語の中には、過去分詞の -ed の部分が発音されない表記になっているものもありますので、英語の発音やつづりを間違えないように気をつけましょう。

## PLUS

# That's where I was born

### Unit 19

関係詞②：関係副詞

## Dialogue  B-62

青色部分に注意しながら会話を聞いてみましょう。

Kaz: Your album is so thick! Let me take a look at some pages. What's this place?

Lisa: Rome. That's where I was born. I lived there until I was six. After that, we moved to Russia.

Kaz: How about this photo? It looks like somewhere in Asia.

Lisa: Yes, I attended a high school in Hong Kong. That was the time when I started to learn Chinese.

Kaz: That's why you can speak Italian, Russian and Chinese so fluently.

Lisa: I had to live in different countries because of my father's job. That's how I learned the three languages.

Kaz: Wow, that's great. I wish I could speak at least two other languages.

## Warm Up  B-63 ▶ 65

英文を聞いて、ダイアログの内容と一致する場合はTを、一致しない場合はFを○で囲みましょう。

1. T / F
2. T / F
3. T / F

# ▶ Tips for Grammar ◀　関係副詞

関係副詞は《前置詞＋関係代名詞》を1語で言い換えることができるもので、where、when、why、how などがあります。

## where
先行詞が「場所」を表す場合に用いられます。

　　The hotel where we stayed was gorgeous.　私たちが泊まったホテルは豪華だった。
　　　= The hotel in which we stayed was gorgeous.
　　Peru is the country where he wants to go.　ペルーは彼の行きたい国だ。
　　　= Peru is the country to which he wants to go.

## when
先行詞が「時」を表す場合に用いられます。

　　I remember the day (when) I entered the elementary school.　私は小学校に入学した日を覚えている。
　　　= I remember the day on which I entered the elementary school.

## why
先行詞が「理由（the reason）」を表す場合に用いられます。

　　Tell us (the reason) why you want to live in a dorm.　なぜ君は寮に住みたいのか、私たちに理由を教えて。
　　　= Tell us (the reason) for which you want to live in a dorm.

## how
先行詞が「方法」を表す場合に用いられます。

　　This is how he's mastered English.　こんなふうに彼は英語をマスターした。
　　　= This is the way (in which) he's mastered English.

⇒詳しくは **124** ページ参照

# Practice 1

（　）に適切な関係副詞を入れましょう。

1. Do you still remember the day (　　　　) we first met?
2. Do you know the country (　　　　) Liz was born?
3. That's (　　　　) I didn't want to go on a trip with her.
4. This is (　　　　) I finished my report in two hours.
5. He forgot the time (　　　　) the meeting would start.
6. This is the place (　　　　) I want to live in the future.

# Practice 2  🎧 B-66　　　Hint p. 124

下の英文はイラストを描写しています。（ ）に適切な語を入れ、音声を聞いて答えを確認しましょう。

1. Spring is the (　　　　) (　　　　　) people enjoy cherry (　　　　　).
2. This is the only place (　　　　) people can (　　　　) drinks.
3. The singer is very famous. (　　　　) (　　　　) he is wearing a mask and (　　　　).
4. He is explaining (　　　　) a math question (　　　　) (　　　　) solved.

# Practice 3  🎧 B-67　　　Hint p. 124

英文には間違いが1つあります。間違いの部分に下線を引いて訂正しましょう。そのあと音声を聞いて答えを確認しましょう。

1. That's the reason how I can't get along with her.
   →

2. There was a time where people were wearing *kimono* every day.
   →

3. Rome is one of the places where I want to go to.
   →

4. We can leave the house wherever you are ready.
   →

5. I remember the day which I had the first date with him.
   →

# Unit 19 That's where I was born

## Practice 4

例を参考にしながら、自分のことについての枠内の文を完成させましょう。

例

The place where I grew up is ( Matsuyama ). It's ( a quiet town ).
I remember the day when ( I met my best friend, Hana ).
( Kobe ) is where I live now.
I really like ( walking ). That's why ( I go mountain climbing very often ).
In the future, I'd like to live in a place where ( there is a lot of nature ).

| |
|---|
| The place where I grew up is (　　　　). It's (　　　　).<br>I remember the day when (　　　　).<br>(　　　　) is where I live now.<br>I really like (　　　　). That's why (　　　　).<br>In the future, I'd like to live in a place where (　　　　). |

## Practice 5

クラスメートと Practice 4 の答えをシェアしましょう。

---

▶ **Grammar in Action** ◀　　歌詞によく使われる関係副詞

歌は英語表現や発音を学ぶうえでの素晴らしい教材となります。ONE OK ROCK の "Wherever You Are" というラブソングを知っていますか。曲のサビの部分に以下のような歌詞があります。

"Wherever you are, I always make you smile. Wherever you are, I'm always by your side."
（君がどこにいても僕がいつも君を笑顔にしてあげるよ。君がどこにいても僕はいつも君のそばにいるよ）

# PLUS

## Unit 20: I shouldn't have done such a stupid thing

仮定法②：仮定法過去完了

## Dialogue  B-69

青色部分に注意しながら会話を聞いてみましょう。

Lisa: What's wrong, Bob? You look down.
Bob: I had a big fight with my girlfriend. She was late for our date, and I shouted at her loudly. I shouldn't have done such a stupid thing.
Lisa: It's really unusual for you to be so angry.
Bob: I know. I had a long day at work yesterday. If I hadn't worked overtime, I wouldn't have been so tired.
Lisa: Don't worry. If you apologize to her from the bottom of your heart, she will forgive you.
Bob: I hope so. I wish I could have had a happy time with her.
Lisa: Why don't you call her right now and say sorry?
Bob: Yeah, I'll do that.

## Warm Up  B-70 ▶ 72

英文を聞いて、ダイアログの内容と一致する場合はTを、一致しない場合はFを○で囲みましょう。

1. T / F
2. T / F
3. T / F

# Unit 20　I shouldn't have done such a stupid thing

## ▶ Tips for Grammar ◀　仮定法過去完了

過去の時点における事実ではないことや実現の可能性がないことを表すときに使われるのが仮定法過去完了です。

**基本形**
《If + 主語 + had + 過去分詞、主語 + would/could + have + 過去分詞》「もし…だったら、〜だっただろうに」
　If I had been in Paris, I could have met you.　もし私がパリにいたらあなたに会えただろうに。

**if 節の否定**
if 節を否定の表現にするときは had を had not [hadn't] とします。
　If I hadn't gone hiking, I wouldn't have caught a cold.　ハイキングに行かなかったら、私は風邪なんか引いていなかっただろうに。

**I wish を使った表現**
《I wish + 主語 + had + 過去分詞》「…だったらよかったのに」
　I wish I had met you when we were younger.　私たちがもっと若いときに君に会っていたらよかったのになあ。
《I wish + 主語 + could have + 過去分詞》「…できたらよかったのに」
　I wish I could have enjoyed the time with her.　彼女との時間を楽しめたらよかったのになあ。

**should を使った表現**
《should have + 過去分詞》「…すべきだったのに」
　I should have apologized to her.　私は彼女に謝るべきだったのだが。

⇒詳しくは 126 ページ参照

## Practice 1

日本語に合うように（　）に適切な語を入れましょう。

1. もっと時間があったら、他のアトラクションも楽しめたのに。
　If we (　　　　) (　　　　　　) more time, we (　　　　　　) (　　　　　　　　) enjoyed other attractions.

2. アルバイトをしていなかったら、一緒に USJ に行けたのに。
　(　　　　　　) I (　　　　　　) (　　　　　　) part-time, I (　　　　　　) (　　　　　　　　)
　(　　　　　　) to USJ with you.

3. 昨日あなたと買い物に行けたらよかったのになあ。
　I (　　　　　　) I (　　　　　　) (　　　　　　) (　　　　　　　) shopping with you yesterday.

4. 重たいスーツケースを空港に送っておくべきだったなあ。
　I (　　　　　　) (　　　　　　) (　　　　　　) my heavy (　　　　　　) to the airport.

## Practice 2  B-73  Hint p. 126

下の英文はイラスト内に矢印で示した人物のセリフです。（　）に適切な語を入れ、音声を聞いて答えを確認しましょう。

1. I (　　　　) my professor (　　　　) (　　　　) in his office when I visited him.
2. I (　　　　) I (　　　　) (　　　　) a fight with my girlfriend.
3. I should (　　　　) (　　　　) my (　　　　).
4. I (　　　　) (　　　　) turned (　　　　) the fan.

## Practice 3  B-74  Hint p. 126

同じ意味になるように、次の文を仮定法過去完了の表現を使って書き換えましょう。そのあと音声を聞いて答えを確認しましょう。

1. We couldn't go shopping because we didn't have enough money.
   →
2. I couldn't wake up early because I stayed up late.
   →
3. I couldn't say hello to him because you were not with me.
   →
4. She missed the bus because her alarm clock was broken.
   →
5. I was late because I overslept.
   →

# Practice 4

例を参考にしながら、先週あったことで「こうしていればよかった」と自分が思うことについて述べる枠内の文を、《should/shouldn't have ＋過去分詞》の表現を使って完成させましょう。

例   B-75

1. I should have woken up earlier on Wednesday.
2. I should have called my family on Saturday.
3. I should have attended the soccer practice on Friday.
4. I shouldn't have forgotten my English homework on Thursday.
5. I shouldn't have been absent from school on Monday.
6. I shouldn't have skipped my lunch on Tuesday.

---

1. I should have ( ).
2. I should have ( ).
3. I should have ( ).
4. I shouldn't have ( ).
5. I shouldn't have ( ).
6. I shouldn't have ( ).

---

# Practice 5

クラスメートと Practice 4 の答えをシェアしましょう。

---

▶ **Grammar in Action** ◀　過去の行為の後悔を表す

過去の行為や行動への後悔の気持ちを表す《should/shouldn't have ＋過去分詞》の表現は会話の中でよく使われます。例えば、映画『ノッティングヒルの恋人』では、主人公のアナが見知らぬ人にひどいことを言ってしまったあと、"I shouldn't have done that."「あんなことするんじゃなかった」と後悔しているシーンがあります。

# Unit 1　名詞
## ▶ More Tips for Grammar ◀

**種類**

❶　数えられる名詞

　普通名詞
　　pen（ペン）、pencil（鉛筆）、book（本）、desk（机）、chair（椅子）、house（家）など。

　集合名詞
　　family（家族）、team（チーム）、club（クラブ）、class（クラス）、staff（スタッフ）、group（集団）、crowd（群衆）など。

❷　数えられない名詞

　物質名詞（決まった形を持たない名詞）
　　coffee（コーヒー）、water（水）、rain（雨）、smoke（煙）、money（お金）、chalk（チョーク）、bread（パン）、cheese（チーズ）、wine（ワイン）、beer（ビール）、paper（紙）など。

　抽象名詞（感情、物の性質、状態などを表す名詞）
　　kindness（親切）、happiness（幸福）、work（仕事）、homework（宿題）、news（ニュース）、information（情報）、advice（アドバイス）など。

**用法**

❸　普通名詞
　There are a table and three chairs in my room.　私の部屋にはテーブル1つと椅子が3脚ある。
　I bought a pen and two notebooks.　私はペン1本とノート2冊を買った。

❹　集合名詞
　Many people gathered in the concert hall.　コンサート会場に多くの人が集まった。
　The police were looking for the criminal.　警察はその犯人を探していた。

❺　物質名詞
　I ordered another glass of beer.　私はビールをもう1杯注文した。
　My mother bought four pieces of chocolate cake.　母はチョコレートケーキを4つ買った。

❻　抽象名詞
　She always gives me a useful piece of advice.　彼女はいつも役立つ忠告を1つしてくれる。

**注意が必要な名詞**

❼　ふつう複数形で用いられる名詞
　pants（パンツ）、trousers（ズボン）、scissors（はさみ）、shoes（靴）、socks（靴下）、contact lenses（コンタクトレンズ）、glasses（眼鏡）などは1つの形状であっても、実際は2つ以上の要素で出来上がっているので複数形が用いられます。
　I bought a pair of jeans and three pairs of socks.　私はジーンズ1本と靴下を3足買った。

# Pair Practice

p. 11 のメニューを見ながら、一人が客、もう一人が店員の立場になって英語で話しましょう。

| | |
|---|---|
| *Waiter/Waitress:* | Have you decided? |
| *Customer:* | Yes. I'd like . . . |
| *Waiter/Waitress:* | How about your main dish? |
| *Customer:* | I'd like to have . . . and . . . , please. |
| *Waiter/Waitress:* | OK, any desserts? |
| *Customer:* | Well, I'll have . . . , please. |

# Unit 2　be 動詞と一般動詞
## ▶ More Tips for Grammar ◀

**be 動詞と一般動詞**

❶　be 動詞

主語によって is、am、are の使い分けが必要です。

Joe is my roommate.　ジョーは私のルームメートだ。

I am an exchange student and a sophomore.　私は交換留学生で大学 2 年生だ。

We are all big fans of the Major Leagues.　私たちはみんなメジャーリーグの大ファンだ。

❷　一般動詞

get、give、take、make、have といった一般動詞を上手に使いこなすと、英語での会話が楽になります。

Please get me a doctor.　お医者さんを呼んでください。

I'll give you a ride.　車に乗せてあげるよ。

I'll have another cup of tea, please.　紅茶をもう 1 杯いただきます。

**自動詞と他動詞**

❸　自動詞

目的語となる名詞や代名詞を必要としない動詞を自動詞と呼びます。なお、自動詞はすぐ後ろに前置詞を伴う場合がよくあります。この場合、前置詞は目的語にはなり得ないので、その前置詞の前にある動詞は他動詞ではありません。注意しましょう。

She never smiles.　彼女は決して微笑まない。

My dog always runs to me.　私の犬はいつも私のところまで走って来る。

❹　他動詞

目的語を必要とする動詞を他動詞と呼びます。

He runs an Italian restaurant.　彼はイタリア料理店を経営している。

She eats fruit every day.　彼女は毎日果物を食べる。

❺　注意が必要な他動詞

marry（…と結婚する）、enter（…に入る）、approach（…に近づく）、attend（…に出席する）、discuss（…について議論する）などは日本語に惑わされて、marry with、enter into、approach to、attend to、discuss about などとしてしまいがちです。しかし、これらの動詞はすべて他動詞なので前置詞は必要なく、すぐ後ろに目的語が来ます。

I attend the staff meeting every Monday.　私は毎週月曜日、スタッフ会議に出席する。

Don't enter the meeting room.　その会議室に入らないで。

I don't want to discuss it anymore.　私はそれについてこれ以上議論したくない。

# Pair Practice

表内の項目に関する自分の情報を英語で書き、下の会話例を参考にしながら、クラスメートとシェアしましょう。

|            | You | Partner 1 | Partner 2 |
|------------|-----|-----------|-----------|
| First Name |     |           |           |
| Last Name  |     |           |           |
| Blood type |     |           |           |
| Major      |     |           |           |
| Hobby      |     |           |           |

### 例

A: What's your ( first name )?
B: (                              ). What's yours?

# Unit 3　前置詞
## ▶ More Tips for Grammar ◀

### over / under / above / below

❶ over「…の上に」（上方を覆っているイメージ）
　A beautiful rainbow is over the buildings.　ビルの上に美しい虹がかかっている。

❷ under「…の下に」（下方に空間が広がっているイメージ）
　She found her glasses under the chair.　彼女は椅子の下でメガネを見つけた。

❸ above「…より上に」（ある基準よりも上）
　The people above us were so noisy last night.　昨夜、上の階の人たちがとても騒がしかった。

❹ below「…より下に」（ある基準よりも下）
　The boat is sinking below the surface of the river.　ボートが川面の下に沈んでいっている。

### between / behind / in front of / next to / across from

❺ between A and B「AとBの間に」
　The restaurant is between the bank and the café.　レストランは銀行とカフェの間にある。

❻ behind「…の裏に」
　The park is behind the department store.　公園はデパートの裏手にある。

❼ in front of「…の前に」
　The bus stop is in front of the department store.　バス停はデパートの前にある。

❽ next to「…の隣に」
　The post office is next to the police station.　郵便局は交番の隣にある。

❾ across from「…から通りを隔てた向かいに」
　The supermarket is across from the café.　スーパーはカフェから通りを隔てた向かいにある。

### to / for / from

❿ to「…へ向かって」
　John went to the convenience store.　ジョンはコンビニエンスストアへ行った。

⓫ for「…の間ずっと、…へ向かって」
　I have been here for almost a month.　私は1か月近くここに滞在している。
　Yoko left for New York.　ヨーコはニューヨークへ向かった。

⓬ from「…から、…出身の」
　It takes about one hour from Tokyo to Osaka by plane.　東京から大阪まで飛行機で約1時間かかる。
　Kathy is from Canada.　キャシーはカナダ出身だ。

### before / after

⓭ before「…より前に」
　My father came home before 11:00 last night.　父は昨夜11時前に帰宅した。

⓮ after「…の後で」
　Let's play basketball after school.　放課後にバスケットボールをしよう。

# Pair Practice

番号がついていないエリアに自由に数字を書き入れましょう。次に、下の会話例を参考にして、前ページの ❺〜❾の表現を使いながらクラスメートと場所の確認をし合いましょう。

1. ~~Department Store~~
2. Convenience Store
3. Police Station
4. ~~Post Office~~
5. Restaurant
6. Park
7. ~~Pond~~
8. ~~Bank~~
9. Café

Your answer

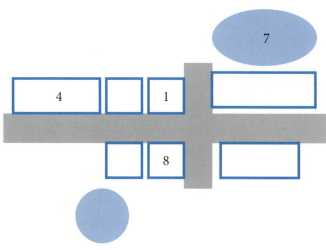

A: Where is the police station?
B: It's . . .

Partner's answer

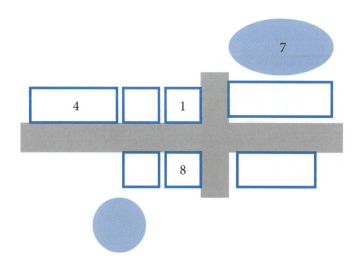

# Unit 4　接続詞
## ▶ More Tips for Grammar ◀

**単語と単語、句と句、節と節をつなぐ接続詞**

❶ and「…そして〜」
　Kaz arrived in New York and he started his new life.　カズはニューヨークに到着して新しい生活を始めた。

❷ but「…しかし〜」
　He said his house was near the station, but it wasn't.　彼の家は駅に近いと言っていたがそうではなかった。

❸ or「…か〜」
　I'll go to Hawaii or Australia this winter.　私はこの冬、ハワイかオーストラリアに行くつもりだ。

**時を表す接続詞**

❹ when / while「…するときに／…する間に」
　I used to play baseball when I was a child.　私は子供の頃、野球をしたものだ。
　I met my old friend while I was waiting for a bus.　バスを待っている間に、私は旧友に会った。

❺ before / after「…する前に／…した後に」
　Please take off your shoes before you enter this room.　この部屋に入る前に靴を脱いでください。
　She learned Japanese after she came to Tokyo.　彼女は東京へ来てから、日本語を学んだ。

**原因・理由・結果を表す接続詞**

❻ because / since「…なので〜」
　He was very upset because I broke the rule.　私が規則を破ったので、彼はとても怒っていた。
　Since we're in Osaka, let's eat *takoyaki*.　大阪にいるんだから、たこ焼きを食べよう。

❼ so「…だから〜」
　You worked very hard, so you'll have a good result.　君はとても熱心に取り組んだから良い結果がもたらされるだろう。

**条件や譲歩を表す接続詞**

❽ though / although「…であるけれども」
　Though I can run fast, I can't swim fast.　私は早く走れるけれども、早くは泳げない。

❾ even if「たとえ…でも」
　Try again even if you fail.　失敗しても、もう一度やってみなさい。

More Tips for Grammar & Pair Practice

# Pair Practice

4枚のイラストを好きな順番に並べ替えて、英語でストーリーを作ってみましょう。その際、枠内の接続詞をいくつか使ってみましょう。

| after | and | because | before | but | or | so | when |

| 順番 | イラスト | 英文 |
|---|---|---|
| 1. | | |
| 2. | | |
| 3. | | |
| 4. | | |

95

# Unit 5　時制①：現在形と現在進行形
## ▶ More Tips for Grammar ◀

**現在形**

❶ 動作動詞を使った現在形
動作を表現する目的で使われるのが動作動詞です。
He visits his grandmother every weekend.　彼は毎週末、祖母を訪ねる。
She takes a piano lesson every Sunday.　毎週日曜日に彼女はピアノのレッスンを受ける。

❷ 状態動詞を使った現在形
同じ状態が続くときに使うのが状態動詞で、ふつう進行形では用いません。状態動詞は次のように分類することができます。
・心理状態を表す：believe、forget、hope、know、like、love、remember、want など。
・感覚を表す：feel、hear、see、smell、taste など。
・その他：belong to、contain、exist、have、own など。
She loves Paris and New York.　彼女はパリとニューヨークを愛している。
Do you remember my name?　私の名前を覚えていますか。
I belong to a tennis club.　私はテニス部に所属している。

❸ 反復動作を表す現在形
継続的に繰り返される動作を表す場合にも現在形を使います。
I always wake up at 7:00.　私はいつも7時に起きる。

❹ 不変の事実や真理を表す現在形
次の例文で述べられているような不変の事実は、過去・現在・未来を通して変わることがないので現在形を使います。また、ことわざや格言の内容はいつの時代でも同じなので、やはり現在形で表します。
The sun sets in the west.　太陽は西に沈む。
Practice makes perfect.　習うより慣れろ。

**現在進行形：《is / am / are + *doing*》**

❺ 進行中の動作を表す現在進行形
繰り返される動作ではなく、今まさに目の前で起こっている動作を表す場合は現在進行形を使います。また今のこの時点だけでなく、一定期間に続けられる動作や、近い将来に行われる予定の動作を表すときにも現在進行形が使われます。
Kaz is running in the park now.　カズは今、公園で走っている。
These days, I am eating a lot of snacks.　最近、私はお菓子をたくさん食べている。
I'm leaving Japan for Canada tonight.　私は今晩カナダに向けて日本を発つことになっている。

# Pair Practice

次の行動内容に関して、自分に当てはまると思われる答えのほうにチェック（✓）を入れ、下の会話例を参考にしてクラスメートとシェアしましょう。

## These Days, I'm...

|  | You | | Partner | |
| --- | --- | --- | --- | --- |
| eating a lot of snacks. | Yes ☐ | No ☐ | Yes ☐ | No ☐ |
| feeling good. | Yes ☐ | No ☐ | Yes ☐ | No ☐ |
| skipping my breakfast. | Yes ☐ | No ☐ | Yes ☐ | No ☐ |
| using my smartphone too much. | Yes ☐ | No ☐ | Yes ☐ | No ☐ |
| studying English hard. | Yes ☐ | No ☐ | Yes ☐ | No ☐ |
| sleeping a lot. | Yes ☐ | No ☐ | Yes ☐ | No ☐ |
| enjoying this textbook. | Yes ☐ | No ☐ | Yes ☐ | No ☐ |

例

A:　Are you eating a lot of snacks these days?
B:　Yes, I think so. How about you?
A:　No, I'm not. Actually, I don't like snacks.

# Unit 6　時制②：過去形と現在完了形
## ▶ More Tips for Grammar ◀

**過去形**

❶ 過去の動作・状態を表す過去形
過去のある時点における動作・状態を述べる際に使われます。
He loved drawing pictures in his childhood.　子供の頃、彼は絵を描くのが大好きだった。
She wasn't very talkative when she was little.　小さい頃、彼女はあまりおしゃべりではなかった。

❷ 過去の反復動作を表す過去形
過去に繰り返し行った動作も過去形で表すことができます。
She usually went to school by bus.　彼女はたいていバスで通学した。
Did you sometimes have lunch with her?　あなたは時々彼女と昼食を共にしましたか。

❸ 過去に１回行われた動作を表す過去形
過去のある時点に１回だけ行われた動作も過去形で表します。
I visited London last summer.　私は去年の夏、ロンドンを訪れた。
I didn't work part-time yesterday.　私は昨日、アルバイトをしなかった。

**現在完了形：《have / has ＋過去分詞》**

❹ 完了・結果を表す現在完了形
これまでやってきたことが終了し、その結果、今どうなっているのか、という状況を表す際に現在完了形を用います。already（すでに）、just（ちょうど）、yet（まだ／もう）といった副詞を伴うことがよくあります。会話の中では I have を I've、He has を He's といった具合に省略した形で使います。
I've just finished my lunch.　私はちょうど昼食を終えたところだ。
He has already gone to America.　彼はもうアメリカに行ってしまった。（今はもういない）
I haven't done my homework yet.　私はまだ宿題をやっていない。

❺ 経験を表す現在完了形
今までにある行為を何回経験したかということを表す際にも現在完了形が使われます。その際は often（しばしば）、once（1度）、twice（2度）、before（以前に）、ever（今までに）、never（一度も…ない）などの副詞を伴います。
I've visited the Grand Canyon twice.　私はグランドキャニオンを２度訪れたことがある。
Have you ever tried Brazilian food?　あなたはブラジル料理を食べてみたことがありますか。

❻ 継続を表す現在完了形
ある状態が過去から現在まで続いてきたことを表す際にも現在完了形を使います。いつの時点から続いているのかを述べる場合が多いので、since（…以来）や for（…の間）などの表現が一緒によく使われます。
They have lived in this town since 1985.　彼らは 1985 年以来、この町に住んでいる。
They have lived in this town for 30 years.　彼らはこの町に 30 年間住んでいる。

# Pair Practice

次の質問に対する自分の答えにチェック（✓）を入れ、下の会話例を参考にしてクラスメートとシェアしましょう。

## Have You Ever...?

|  | You | | Partner | |
| --- | --- | --- | --- | --- |
| been to any foreign countries? | Yes ☐ | No ☐ | Yes ☐ | No ☐ |
| tried snowboarding? | Yes ☐ | No ☐ | Yes ☐ | No ☐ |
| been to any rock concerts? | Yes ☐ | No ☐ | Yes ☐ | No ☐ |
| read any novels written by Keigo Higashino? | Yes ☐ | No ☐ | Yes ☐ | No ☐ |
| met any movie stars or music stars? | Yes ☐ | No ☐ | Yes ☐ | No ☐ |

A: Have you ever been to any foreign countries?
B: Yes. I've been to Hawaii. / No. I've never . . .

# Unit 7　時制③：未来形
## ▶ More Tips for Grammar ◀

❶ will を使った未来形
will については、以下のように自然の成り行きで起こる場合と、話し手の意思を表す場合の 2 つの使い方があります。
My grandfather will be ninety next month.　祖父は来月 90 歳になる。
I will call you tonight.　今晩電話するよ。
I won't go to the party tomorrow.　私は明日のパーティーには行かない。

❷ be going to を使った未来形
《be going to ＋動詞の原形》で表す未来形は、以前からすでに決まっている予定を述べる場合や、話し手がこれからそうなるだろうと判断している事柄を述べる場合に用いられます。
I am going to go grocery shopping.　私は食料品の買い出し行くつもりだ。
Bring your umbrella. It's going to rain.　傘を持って行きなさい。雨が降りそうだから。
Are you going to take the psychology class?　あなたは心理学の授業を履修するつもりですか。
He's not going to come back to Japan in summer.　彼は夏に日本に戻ってくる予定はない。

❸ 現在形で未来の時制を表す
列車の発着時刻やすでに予定に入っている事柄など、現時点で変更の可能性がない未来の事柄の場合は、未来に生じることであっても現在形で表すことができます。
The train leaves for Osaka at 15:10.　その電車は 15 時 10 分に大阪へ出発する。
The team begins winter training in January.　そのチームは 1 月に冬季トレーニングを始める。

❹ 進行形で未来の時制を表す
現時点において未来の出来事に向けて準備を進めている場合には、現在進行形を使って、その未来の出来事を表すことができます。
He is leaving for Canada next week.　彼は来週カナダへ出発する。
We are holding a school festival next month.　来月、学園祭がある。

❺ その他の未来の時制を表す表現
今まさに起ころうとしている状況を表すには、《be about to ＋動詞の原形》を使います。
Hurry. The movie is about to start.　急いで。映画が始まるよ。
すでに決まっている公式の予定などを述べるときには、《be to ＋ 動詞の原形》を使います。
The U.S. President is to visit Japan next month.　米国大統領は来月訪日する予定だ。

# Pair Practice

質問に対する自分の答えを書いて、クラスメートとシェアしましょう。

## What Will You Do If...?

|  | You | Partner |
|---|---|---|
| it starts raining suddenly on the way home? | | |
| your best friend calls you "stupid"? | | |
| you find 10,000 yen on the street? | | |
| have a fight with your parents? | | |
| you forget to bring your wallet? | | |
| you lose your cell phone or smartphone? | | |

**例**

A:  What will you do if it starts raining suddenly on the way home?
B:  I will buy an umbrella at a convenience store. How about you?
A:  I will . . .

# Unit 8　助動詞①：can / may
## ▶ More Tips for Grammar ◀

### can

❶ 能力・可能を表す can / be able to

John can sing well but he can't play any musical instruments.　ジョンはうまく歌えるが、楽器は何も弾けない。

I can see you any time after lunch.　昼食後であればいつでも君に会えるよ。

Kaz will be able to enjoy his new life in New York soon.　カズはすぐにニューヨークでの新しい生活を楽しめるようになるだろう。

❷ 許可を表す can

You can choose either tea or coffee.　紅茶かコーヒーのどちらかを選ぶことができます。

You can't eat in the library.　図書館では食事はできません。

Can I turn on the air conditioner?　エアコンをつけてもいいですか。

❸ 依頼を表す can

誰かに何かを頼むときは、Can you...? と尋ねるのが一般的です。より丁寧な言い方をする場合は、Could you...? となります。

Can you help me with the dishes?　洗い物を手伝ってもらえませんか。

Could you tell me how I can get to the station?　駅への行き方を教えていただけませんか。

❹ 可能性を表す can

can を使うと「…はあり得る」という可能性を示唆することになります。

Don't worry. Anyone can make mistakes.　心配しないで。誰でも間違うことはあるから。

❺ 確信を表す can't

「…のはずがない」との強い確信を持っている場合は can't / cannnot を使ってその意味合いを表すことができます。

The story can't be true.　その話は本当のはずがない。

### may

❻ 許可を表す may

「…してもよいですか」と相手に許可を求める場合は、May I...? という表現を使います。may の否定形である may not は「…してはいけない」という不許可を表し、強い禁止のニュアンスを含むこともあります。

May I use your computer?　あなたのコンピュータを使ってもよろしいですか。

You may not come in without permission.　許可なしに入ってはいけません。

❼ 推量を表す may / might

may や might は「…かもしれない」という推量を表します。might は may よりも可能性が低い場合に使われます。

She may not be at home now.　彼女は今、家にいないかもしれない。

He might come to the party tonight.　今夜、彼はパーティーに来るかもしれない。

# Pair Practice

高校時代の校則を思い出して各項目にチェック（✓）を入れ、下の会話例を参考にクラスメートとシェアしましょう。

## Could or Couldn't

|  | You | | Partner | |
| --- | --- | --- | --- | --- |
| perm your hair | Yes ☐ | No ☐ | Yes ☐ | No ☐ |
| work part-time | Yes ☐ | No ☐ | Yes ☐ | No ☐ |
| get a driver's license | Yes ☐ | No ☐ | Yes ☐ | No ☐ |
| wear casual clothes | Yes ☐ | No ☐ | Yes ☐ | No ☐ |

A: Could you perm your hair while at high school?
B: No, I couldn't. How about your school?

# Unit 9 　助動詞② : could / would
## ▶ More Tips for Grammar ◀

### could

❶ 可能性を表す could

could は「…かもしれない」という可能性を表す際に使われます。つづりは過去形ですが、意味的には現在のことを表すので注意しましょう。否定形の couldn't は「…のはずがない」という意味になります。

She could have a second house.　彼女は別荘を持っているかもしれない。
She couldn't be an actress.　彼女は女優であるはずがない。

### would

❷ 推量を表す would

確信の度合いが低く、「たぶん…だろう」と言うときに would を用います。will よりも控えめで丁寧な感じになります。この場合もつづりは過去形ですが、意味的には現在のことを表します。

That would be the best plan.　それがたぶん最良の計画だろう。

❸ 過去の時点での拒絶を表す would

「どうしても…しようとしなかった」という過去の時点における拒絶を表します。

Mike wouldn't clean up his room.　マイクはどうしても部屋を掃除しようとはしなかった。

❹ 過去の習慣を表す would

would は「よく…したものだ」という過去における習慣やくり返し行われた動作を表すときにも用いられます。

My father and I would often play catch when I was a boy.　子供の頃、父と私はよくキャッチボールをしたものだ。

❺ 依頼を表す would

「…していただけませんか」と丁寧に依頼をする際には Would you...? という表現を使います。Will you...? という言い方をするとややぞんざいに響くことがあるので、初対面の人や目上の人には Would you...? を用いるほうが無難です。

Would you close the door, please?　ドアを閉めていただけませんか。

❻ 要望を表す would

would like to... の形を用いると「…したいと思います」という丁寧な表現になります。友人同士であれば want to... でも構いませんが、初対面の人や目上の人には would like to... を使って自分の要望を丁寧に伝えましょう。

I would like to attend the meeting.　会議に出席したいのですが。

# Pair Practice

自分が週末に行きたい場所とそこでやりたいことをそれぞれ表の Where と What の欄に書き入れ、下の会話例を参考にクラスメートとシェアしましょう。

## Weekend Activities

|           | Where | What |
|-----------|-------|------|
| You       |       |      |
| Partner 1 |       |      |
| Partner 2 |       |      |
| Partner 3 |       |      |
| Partner 4 |       |      |
| Partner 5 |       |      |

**例**

A: Where would you like to go this weekend?
B: I'd like to go to a shopping center. I'd like to buy . . . How about you?
A: I'd like to . . .

# Unit 10　助動詞③：should / must / have to / had better
## ▶ More Tips for Grammar ◀

### must

❶ must の疑問文
　疑問文を作るときは、can や may の場合と同じように must を文頭に出して作りますが、must を用いた疑問文を実際に使う場面は限られます。
　Must I apologize to her?　私は彼女に謝らなければなりませんか。

❷ must の否定形
　must not もしくは mustn't の形で強い禁止を表し、「…してはいけない」という意味になります。
　You mustn't smoke here.　ここでタバコを吸ってはいけない。

❸ 強い確信を表す must
　周囲の状況から間違いなく「…に違いない」と断定するときにも must が使われます。
　She must be an actress.　彼女は女優に違いない。

❹ 強い勧めを表す must
　親しい間柄では、「ぜひ…してね」という意味合いで must が使われることがあります。
　You must come and see me.　ぜひ私に会いに来て下さい。

### have to

❺ have to の疑問文
　《Do / Does ＋主語＋ have to...?》の形で「…しなければならないか」という意味になります。
　Do I have to get on that train?　私はあの電車に乗らないといけないのかな。
　Does he have to attend Professor Tani's lecture?　彼は谷教授の講義に出席しないといけませんか。

❻ have to の否定文
　《don't / doesn't have to...》の形で「…する必要はない、…しなくてもよい」という意味になります。must not（…してはいけない）との意味の違いに注意しましょう。
　You don't have to get up early tomorrow morning.　明日の朝は早く起きなくてもいいよ。

### should / ought to

❼ 義務を表す should / ought to
　should も ought to もほぼ同じ意味で使われ、「…すべきだ」という意味になります。同じ意味の日本語ほど強制的でなく、「…するほうがよい」といった忠告のニュアンスを含む助動詞です。
　You should eat breakfast every day.　あなたは毎日朝食を食べるべきだ。
　We ought to help with each other.　私たちはお互い助け合うべきだ。

### had better

❽ 忠告を表す had better
　had better には「…したほうがよい」という意味の他に、「…しなさい」という強い意味があるので、初対面の人や目上の人に対しては使わないほうが無難です。
　You'd better see a dentist.　歯医者さんに診てもらいなさい。

# Pair Practice

自分の通った中学校の規則を英語で紹介してみましょう。表の中のフレーズを使って規則を書き出し、下の会話例を参考にしてクラスメートとシェアしましょう。

## My School Regulations

| I had to | |
|---|---|
| I didn't have to | |

A: In my junior high school, I had to wear a uniform, but I didn't have to wear white socks. How about you?

B: In my junior high school, I had to...

# Unit 11　受動態
## ▶ More Tips for Grammar ◀

**受動態の様々な形**

❶　「…によって」を by 以外の前置詞で表す場合
　　The top of Mt Fuji is covered with snow.　富士山頂は雪に覆われている。
　　The fashion designer is known to the world.　そのファッションデザイナーは世界に知られている。
　　My suitcase was filled with souvenirs.　私のスーツケースはお土産で一杯だった。

❷　助動詞と一緒に使う場合：《助動詞＋ be ＋過去分詞》
　　This car must be bought by him next month.　来月、この車は彼によって購入されるに違いない。
　　This tree may be cut down soon.　この木はもうすぐ切り倒されるかもしれない。
　　The problem can't be solved.　その問題は解決されるはずがない。

❸　進行形：《be 動詞＋ being ＋過去分詞》
　　This tower is being built.　このタワーは建設中である。
　　When I came back to my hotel room, it was being cleaned.　私がホテルの部屋に戻ってくると、清掃中だった。

❹　現在完了形：《have / has ＋ been ＋過去分詞》
　　The date of the meeting has been fixed.　ミーティングの日取りは決められている。
　　All flights have been canceled.　全てのフライトがキャンセルされた。

❺　get を使った受動態：《get ＋過去分詞》
　　be 動詞の代わりに get を使うと「…になった」という変化の意味合いを表します。
　　My iPhone was broken.　私の iPhone は壊れていた。
　　My iPhone got broken.　私の iPhone が壊れた。
　　Luckily, nobody got hurt in the accident.　幸いなことにその事故では誰もけがをしなかった。

❻　感情や心理状態を表す受動態
　　感情的・心理的な作用を受ける受動態の場合は by 以外の前置詞がよく使われるので、慣用句として覚えましょう。
　　I was surprised at the news.　私はそのニュースに驚いた。
　　I'm fascinated with his fashion.　私は彼のファッションに魅了されている。
　　I'm tired of listening to jazz.　私はジャズを聞き飽きた。
　　She was disappointed with the movie.　彼女はその映画にがっかりした。
　　I'm excited about the trip to Nagano.　私は長野への旅行にわくわくしている。
　　He's satisfied with his new part-time job.　彼は新しいアルバイトに満足している。

# Pair Practice

表内の例にならって、クイズの答えとして適するものを下の枠内から選んで書き入れましょう。それぞれの選択肢は一度しか使えません。なお、(1) の動詞は過去分詞に変えて記入しましょう。次に、会話例を参考にしながら、受動態を使ってクラスメートと答えをチェックし合ってみましょう。

### Trivia Quiz: By Who?

|  | (1) | (2) |
|---|---|---|
| 例  "Material Girl" | sung | Madonna |
| 例  Horyu-ji | built | Shotoku Taishi |
| Apple Inc. | | |
| Mickey Mouse | | |
| *Monna Lisa* | | |
| *Star Wars Episode 1* | | |
| the *Harry Potter* series | | |

| (1) | build    cook    direct    found    make    paint    sing    write |
|---|---|
| (2) | George Lucas    J. K. Rowling    Leonardo da Vinci    Madonna    Pablo Picasso    Shotoku Taishi    Steve Jobs    Steven Spielberg    Walt Disney |

A: I think "Material Girl" was [ sung ] by ( Madonna ).
B: Yes, I agree. And Horyu-ji was [ built ] by ( Shotoku Taishi ).

# Unit 12　不定詞①：基本用法
## ▶ More Tips for Grammar ◀

**to 不定詞の副詞的用法**
to 不定詞の副詞的用法は「目的」「結果」「原因」などを表します。

❶ 目的を表す：「…するために」
　He is studying hard to be a tour conductor.　ツアーコンダクターになるために彼は熱心に勉強している。
　My boyfriend came from Canada to see me.　ボーイフレンドは、私に会うためにカナダから来てくれた。
　I eat vegetables every day to keep healthy.　私は健康を保つために毎日野菜を食べている。

❷ 結果を表す：「…して」「…した結果〜」
　I woke up to find myself in the hospital.　目が覚めたら私は自分が病院にいることに気づいた。
　I ran to the station, only to miss the 8:00 train.　私は駅まで走ったが、結局8時の電車に乗り遅れた。

❸ 原因や根拠を表す：「…なので」「…するとは」
　I was surprised to see her in Seoul.　彼女にソウルで会うとは驚いた。
　She must be out of her mind to shout at you.　君に大声で叫ぶなんて、彼女は正気じゃないよ。
　He must be a genius to solve the question.　その問題を解くなんて彼は天才に違いない。

**to 不定詞の否定形**

❹ 否定表現の配置
　not や never などの語を to の直前に置きます。
　I catch the 7:00 train not to be late for school.　学校に遅れないように私は7時の電車に乗る。
　I decided not to marry him.　私は彼と結婚しないことに決めた。
　He went to Spain, never to come back.　彼はスペインに行って二度と帰ってこなかった。

**it を仮主語や仮目的語として使った to 不定詞の構文**

❺ to 不定詞の代わりに it を仮の主語や目的語として用いる場合
　to 不定詞を主語や目的語として用いるときは、まず it で代用し、後ろに本来の to 不定詞を続けます。
　また、to 不定詞の意味上の主語はふつう for ＋人で表し、to 不定詞の前に置かれます。
　It is not easy to ride a unicycle.　一輪車に乗るのは簡単ではない。
　I found it interesting to learn Spanish.　スペイン語を学ぶことは面白いとわかった。
　It is necessary for you to pass the test.　あなたにとってその試験に合格することが必要だ。

❻ 人物評価に関わる形容詞が入る場合
　nice、sweet、polite、rude、smart などのように、to 不定詞の意味上の主語の人物を評価する形容詞が使われる場合、for でなく of を用い、その主語は of ＋人で表します。
　It is nice of you to give me a present.　プレゼントをくれるなんてなんてあなたは優しいのかしら。
　It is smart of you to get such a high score.　そんなに高い点数を取るなんて君は賢いね。

# Pair Practice

下の会話例を参考に、クラスメートに次の6つの質問をしてみましょう。

| Question | Answer | |
|---|---|---|
| 1. Is it easy for you to get up early in the morning? | Yes ☐ | No ☐ |
| 2. Is it difficult for you to finish everything on time? | Yes ☐ | No ☐ |
| 3. Is it fun for you to meet a lot of people? | Yes ☐ | No ☐ |
| 4. Is it important for you to get good grades? | Yes ☐ | No ☐ |
| 5. Is it necessary for you to work part-time? | Yes ☐ | No ☐ |
| 6. Is it relaxing for you to take a bath? | Yes ☐ | No ☐ |

A: Is it easy for you to get up early in the morning?
B: No. It's very difficult for me to get up early. How about you?
A: Well, for me, it's not difficult.

# Unit 13　比較
## ▶ More Tips for Grammar ◀

**語形変化**

❶ 比較級・最上級の規則変化と不規則変化

|  | 原級（元の形） | 比較級「～より…」 | 最上級「最も…」 |
|---|---|---|---|
| -er / -est をつける | old | older | oldest |
| y を i に変えて -er / -est をつける | heavy | heavier | heaviest |
| 最後の子音字を重ねて -er / -est をつける | big | bigger | biggest |
| more / most を前に置く（2 音節の語の一部） | careful | **more** careful | **most** careful |
| more / most を前に置く（3 音節以上の語） | difficult | **more** difficult | **most** difficult |
| 不規則変化 | good/well | better | best |
| 不規則変化 | many/much | more | most |
| 不規則変化 | little | less | least |

**比較表現**

❷ 原級：《A ... as ＋形容詞／副詞の原形 ＋ as B》「A は B と同じくらい～」
　Chinese is as difficult as Russian.　中国語はロシア語と同じくらい難しい。
　My room is not as tidy as my sister's.　私の部屋は妹の部屋ほどきちんと片付いていない。
　Kaz can eat as quickly as me / I.　カズは僕と同じくらい速く食べることができる。
　I can't dance as beautifully as Lisa.　私はリサのように美しく踊れない。

❸ 比較級：《A ... 形容詞／副詞の比較級 +than B》「A は B よりも～」
　Living in the dorm is safer than living alone.　1 人暮らしより寮に住むほうが安全だ。
　Steak is more expensive than pizza.　ステーキはピザより高い。
　I can think more positively than my friends.　私は友達よりもポジティブに考えることができる。
　No other girl in her class is kind**er** than Lisa.　リサよりも親切な女の子はクラスにいない。
　She can speak English much better than me.　彼女は私よりもはるかに上手に英語が話せる。
　※「はるかに［ずっと］～」と表現するときは very ではなくて much や far を使います。

❹ 最上級：《形容詞／副詞の最上級 + in / of / among...》「…の中で最も～」
　Kay is the tallest of the three.　ケイは 3 人の中でいちばん背が高い。
　This is the most expensive restaurant in my town.　ここは私の町で最も高級なレストランだ。
　My mother wakes up earliest in my family.　母は家族の中で一番早起きだ。
　Who ate the most in the restaurant yesterday?　昨日レストランで誰が一番多く食べたの？

# Pair Practice

表内の例を参考にし、比較級と最上級の表現を使ってクイズを5問作りましょう。そして、下の会話例にならってクラスメートにクイズを出し合いましょう。

### Trivia Quiz

| | |
|---|---|
| 例1 | What is the highest mountain in the world? |
| 例2 | Which is larger, Lake Biwa or Awaji Island? |
| Q1 | |
| Q2 | |
| Q3 | |
| Q4 | |
| Q5 | |

### 例1

A: What is the highest mountain in the world?
B: It's Everest.

### 例2

A: Which is larger, Lake Biwa or Awaji Island?
B: Lake Biwa is larger.

# Unit 14　関係詞①：関係代名詞
## ▶ More Tips for Grammar ◀

❶ 主格：先行詞が人の場合は who / that、人以外の場合は which / that
　The woman is very kind. She lives next door.　その女性はとても親切だ。彼女は隣に住んでいる。
　→ The woman who lives next door is very kind.　隣に住んでいる女性はとても親切だ。

❷ 所有格：whose
　I have a friend. His brother is a world-famous dancer.　私にはある友達がいる。その友達の兄は世界的に有名なダンサーだ。
　→ I have a friend whose brother is a world-famous dancer.　私にはお兄さんが世界的に有名なダンサーの友達がいる。

❸ 目的格（省略可）：先行詞が人の場合は whom / who / that、人以外の場合は which / that
　I'm watching a DVD. I borrowed it from my friend.　私はある DVD を見ている。その DVD は友達から借りた。
　→ I'm watching a DVD ( which ) I borrowed from my friend.　私は友達から借りた DVD を見ている。

❹ that が使われるケース
　a. 先行詞に特定の語句（the only、the first、the last、all、every、no）や形容詞の最上級表現などが付いている場合
　　This is the best steak that I've ever had.　これは私が今まで食べた中で最高のステーキだ。
　　The only student that got a perfect score was Hiromi.　満点をとった唯一の学生はヒロミだった。
　b. 先行詞が「人＋人」以外の場合
　　This story is about a boy and his dog that travel together.　この物語は共に旅をする少年と犬についてのものだ。

❺ 前置詞＋目的格の関係代名詞
　This is the artist. I was looking for him.　こちらがそのアーティストである。私は彼を探していた。
　→ This is the artist for whom I was looking.　こちらが私の探していたアーティストだ。
　＝ This is the artist ( whom ) I was looking for.（前置詞を最後に置いてもよい）
　This is the house. We live in the house.　これがその家だ。私たちはその家に住んでいる。
　→ This is the house in which we live.　これは私たちが住んでいる家だ。
　＝ This is the house ( which ) we live in.
　※前置詞が関係代名詞の前に置かれるときには、その関係代名詞を省略することができない。

# Pair Practice

次のクイズの答えを書き入れましょう。そのあと下の会話例を参考にして、クラスメートと答え合わせをしましょう。

## What's His/Her Name?

| Quiz | Answer |
|---|---|
| 1. What's the name of the person who wrote the *Tale of Genji*? | |
| 2. What's the name of the person who directed *Princess Mononoke*? | |
| 3. What's the name of the Japanese skater who won the gold medal in the 2014 and 2018 Olympics? | |
| 4. What's the name of the Japanese group who sings "Heavy Rotation"? | |
| 5. What's the name of the Japanese tennis player who reached the best 8 in 2018 Wimbledon? | |

A: What's the name of the person who wrote the *Tale of Genji*?
B: I know the answer. It's (　　　　　　　　　　).
　［別解］ Well, I don't remember. Can you give me some hints?

# Unit 15　仮定法①：仮定法過去
## ▶ More Tips for Grammar ◀

**仮定法過去：実現の可能性がない場合、非現実的な場合**

❶　基本形：《If ＋主語＋(助)動詞の過去形 , 主語＋ would / could / might ＋動詞の原形》「もし…ならば、～するのに」

　　If I had a big sister, I could exchange clothes with her.　私に姉がいたなら服を交換できるのに。
　　If I could be anybody, I would be a famous model.　もし私が誰にでもなれるなら、有名モデルになるわ。
　　If you found 1,000,000 yen on the street, what would you do with the money?　通りで 100 万円を見つけたら、あなたはそのお金をどうする？

❷　if 節内の be 動詞
　　if 節内の主語が I / he / she / it の場合、be 動詞には were を使います（口語では was も可能）。
　　If I were/was Chinese, I could speak Chinese much better.　もし私が中国人なら中国語をもっと上手に話せるのに。
　　If it were/was sunny, we could go to the beach.　もし晴れていれば、私たちはビーチに行けるのに。

❸　if 節が後ろにくる場合
　　I would cry if I won the first prize.　もし 1 等賞をとったら、私はきっと泣くわ。
　　What would you do if you won 10,000,000 yen?　1 千万円当たったら、あなたは何をする？

❹　I wish を使った表現：《I wish ＋主語＋(助)動詞の過去形》「…ならいいのに」「…できたらいいのに」
　　I wish I could talk with animals.　私が動物と話すことができたらいいのに。
　　I wish I were a genius.　自分が天才だったらいいのに。

❺　if 節が省略される場合
　　(If I were you,) I wouldn't give up on my dreams so easily.　私だったらそんな簡単に夢をあきらめないわ。

**仮定法現在：実現の可能性が十分にある場合、現実的な場合**

❻　基本形：《If ＋主語＋(助)動詞の現在形 , 主語＋助動詞＋動詞の原形》「もし…なら～する」
　　If I wake up at 8:00, I can catch the 9:00 train.　8 時に起きれば、9 時の電車に間に合う。
　　If you have a fever, you should go home now.　熱があるなら、すぐ家に帰ったほうがいいよ。
　　What will you do if it rains tomorrow?　明日雨が降ったらあなたは何をする？

❼　仮定法過去と仮定法現在を使い分けるポイント
　　仮定法過去と仮定法現在のどちらを使うかは、話し手がどれくらい実現の可能性があると考えているかによって決まります。
　　If it snows tomorrow, I'll make a snowman.　明日雪が降れば私は雪だるまを作る。
　　If it snowed, I could go skiing.　雪が降れば、私はスキー行けるのに。

# Pair Practice

次の質問に対する自分の答えを書き、下の会話例を参考にしながらクラスメートとシェアしましょう。

| Question | You | Partner |
| --- | --- | --- |
| 1. If you could be a celebrity, who would you be? | | |
| 2. If you could live anywhere in the world, where would you live? | | |
| 3. If you had a time machine, would you go to the future or past? | | |
| 4. If you could choose any job, what job would you choose? | | |
| 5. If you could be reborn, would you be a man or a woman? | | |
| 6. If you could keep any animal, what animal would you choose? | | |
| 7. If you had Aladdin's lamp, what would you ask for? | | |

A: If you could live anywhere in the world, where would you live?
B: I would ( live in Canada ). How about you?
A: I would ( live in Australia ).

# Unit 16　動名詞
## ▶ More Tips for Grammar ◀

❶ 動名詞の否定形
not や never を動名詞の前に置きます。
Not saying "Thank you" is impolite.　「ありがとう」と言わないのは失礼だ。
I'm proud of never being late for school.　決して学校に遅刻しないのを私は誇りに思っている。

❷ 文の主語と動名詞の意味上の主語が異なる場合
動名詞の前に代名詞の所有格か目的格を置くことによって、文脈を明確にします。
I don't like his/him talking bad about you.　彼が君のことを悪く言うのを私は好きではない。
I'm sure of your/you passing the exam.　あなたが試験に合格することを私は確信している。

❸ 動名詞を使った慣用表現
以下の慣用表現には to の後に動名詞が使われています。to 不定詞の一部と混同しないように注意しましょう。
look forward to *doing*「…するのを楽しみにする」
　I look forward to seeing you soon.　君にもうすぐ会えるのを楽しみにしている。
be used to *doing*「…するのに慣れている」
　I'm used to living by myself.　私は一人暮らしに慣れている。

❹ 目的語としての動名詞と to 不定詞
動名詞だけを目的語としてとる動詞：avoid、dislike、enjoy、finish、imagine、keep、miss、practice など。
　例）〇 I practice singing every day.　私は毎日歌う練習をする。
　　　× I practice to sing every day.
to 不定詞だけを目的語としてとる動詞：choose、decide、expect、hope、manage、promise、want など。
　例）〇 I decided to study abroad.　私は留学することに決めた。
　　　× I decided studying abroad.
動名詞か to 不定詞かによって意味が変わる動詞：forget、regret、remember、stop、try など
I stopped to talk with my friend on my smartphone.　私は友達とスマホで電話するために立ち止まった。
I stopped talking with my friend on my smartphone.　私は友達とスマホで電話するのをやめた。

---

I forgot to call my mother.　私は母に電話するのを忘れた。　※未来の行為について
I forgot calling my mother.　私は母に電話したことを忘れた。　※過去の行為について

# Pair Practice

質問に対する自分の答えと理由を書き、下の会話例を参考にしてクラスメートとシェアしましょう。

## Which Do You Like Better?

| Question | Answer | Reason |
| --- | --- | --- |
| 1. Which do you like better, playing sports or watching sports? | | |
| 2. Which do you like better, watching movies at a movie theater or watching DVDs at home? | | |
| 3. Which do you like better, eating bread with jam or butter? | | |
| 4. Which do you like better, listening to music or watching TV? | | |
| 5. Which do you like better, taking a shower or taking a bath? | | |
| 6. Which do you like better, staying up late or waking up early? | | |

**例**

A: Which do you like better, playing sports or watching sports?
B: I like playing sports better because (　　　　　　　　). How about you?
A: I like watching sports better because (　　　　　　　　).

# Unit 17　不定詞②：応用構文と原形不定詞
## ▶ More Tips for Grammar ◀

❶ 《疑問詞＋ to 不定詞》
　I don't know what to say.　なんて言っていいかわからない。
　Do you know where to get a discount ticket?　どこで割引券がもらえるか知ってる？
　Can you tell me how to get to the station?　駅までの行き方を教えてもらえる？
　I wonder which cake to choose.　どちらのケーキを選ぼうかしら。
　Let me know when to visit your house.　いつあなたの家を訪問すればいいか知らせてね。

❷ 《too ＋形容詞＋ to 不定詞》「…すぎて〜できない」
　He is too young to get a driver's license.　彼は運転免許を取るには若すぎる。
　This bag is too heavy to carry.　このかばんは重すぎて運べない。
　This book was too difficult for me to read.　この本は私には難しすぎて読めなかった。

❸ 《形容詞＋ enough ＋ to 不定詞》「…するのに十分〜だ」
　He is old enough to drink alcohol.　彼はアルコールを飲むのに十分な年齢だ。
　She was kind enough to lend me some money.　彼女は親切にもお金を貸してくれた。

❹ 《seem / appear ＋ to 不定詞》「…のようだ、…らしい」　※現在時制
　The foreigner seems to understand Japanese.　その外国人は日本語を理解しているようだ。
　The boy appears to be disappointed.　その少年はがっかりしているようだ。
　He didn't seem to be in trouble.　彼は困っているようではなかった。

❺ 《seem / appear ＋ to have ＋過去分詞》「…したようだ、…したらしい」　※過去時制
　My daughter seems to have gone to school.　娘はもう学校に行ったようだ。
　They appear to have understood me.　彼らは私のことを理解したようだ。

❻ 慣用的に使われる to 不定詞の表現
　To tell (you) the truth, I don't like my father.　実は、私は父のことを好きではない。
　To make matters worse, it began to rain.　さらに困ったことには、雨が降り出した。
　To begin with, you should quit smoking.　まず第一に、あなたはタバコをやめるべきだ。

# Pair Practice

あなたの出身地を訪れる観光客へのアドバイスを、表内の例にならって記入しましょう。そのあと、下の会話例を参考にしてクラスメートとシェアしましょう。

|  | Hometown | Where to Go | What to Eat | What to Buy |
|---|---|---|---|---|
| 例 | Kobe | Mt. Rokko | beef | cookies |
| You |  |  |  |  |
| Partner 1 |  |  |  |  |
| Partner 2 |  |  |  |  |
| Partner 3 |  |  |  |  |

### 例

A: Where are you from?
B: I'm from (          ).
A: Can you tell me where to go [ what to eat / what to buy ] if I visit your hometown?
B: You should go to (          ), eat (          ), and buy (          ).

# Unit 18　分詞
## ▶ More Tips for Grammar ◀

❶ 形容詞として一般化している現在分詞と過去分詞
現在分詞（…させる）と過去分詞（…された）の意味合いを混同しないよう注意しましょう。
excite「わくわくさせる」
　　The new project is exciting.　新しいプロジェクトはわくわくする。
　　He is excited about the new project.　彼は新しいプロジェクトにわくわくしている。
disappoint「がっかりさせる」
　　The movie was disappointing.　その映画はがっかりするようなものだった。
　　I was disappointed with the movie.　私はその映画にがっかりした。

このように形容詞としてよく使われる現在分詞と過去分詞はたくさんあるので覚えておきましょう。

| 元の動詞 | 現在分詞 | 過去分詞 | 元の動詞 | 現在分詞 | 過去分詞 |
|---|---|---|---|---|---|
| amaze | amazing | amazed | embarrass | embarrassing | embarrassed |
| amuse | amusing | amused | interest | interesting | interested |
| annoy | annoying | annoyed | satisfy | satisfying | satisfied |
| bore | boring | bored | shock | shocking | shocked |
| confuse | confusing | confused | terrify | terrifying | terrified |
| depress | depressing | depressed | worry | worrying | worried |

❷ 分詞構文
接続詞を使うことなく、分詞を使った表現を主に文の前に置くことによって情報を付け足す用法です。
以下は、現在分詞を使った慣用的な分詞構文の例です。

frankly speaking「率直に言えば」　　　　generally speaking「一般的に言えば」
strictly speaking「厳密に言えば」　　　　speaking of...「…と言えば」
judging from...「…から判断すると」　　　according to...「…によると」

　　Frankly speaking, this movie isn't interesting.　率直に言えば、この映画は面白くない。
　　Speaking of vegetables, I like carrots.　野菜と言えば、私はニンジンが好きだ。
　　Judging from his accent, he must be Australian.　彼のアクセントから判断すると、彼はオーストラリア人に違いない。
　　According to their study, the Japanese economy will improve.　彼らの研究によると、日本経済は良くなるだろう。

# Pair Practice

以下の質問に Yes と答えたクラスメートの名前を書きましょう。動詞が現在形の場合は Do you...?、過去形の場合は Did you...? で尋ねましょう。

## Find a Person Who...

| Question | Name |
| --- | --- |
| likes relaxing music. | |
| ate fried chicken yesterday. | |
| likes boiled eggs better than scrambled eggs. | |
| had an exciting weekend. | |
| has an amusing friend. | |
| likes iced coffee better than hot coffee. | |
| heard shocking news last night. | |
| enjoys watching animated movies. | |

**例**

A: Do you like relaxing music?
B: Yes / No. Did you eat fried chicken yesterday?
A: Yes / No. . . .

# Unit 19　関係詞②：関係副詞
## ▶ More Tips for Grammar ◀

**関係副詞**

❶ where：場所を表す

This is the place where I was born.　ここが私の生まれた場所だ。

= This is where I was born.　（※先行詞となる the place は省略可能）

❷ when：時間を表す

2017 was the year when I moved to Hawaii.　2017年は私がハワイに移った年だ。

April is the month when the new school year starts in Japan.　（※先行詞は省略可能）

　　　　　　　　　　　　　　　　　　　　　　　　　　　日本では、4月は新年度が始まる月だ。

❸ why：理由を表す

This is the reason why I decided to be a pilot.　これが私がパイロットになろうと決心した理由だ。

= This is why I decided to be a pilot.

❹ how：方法を表す

This is how I became happy.　こんなふうにして私は幸せになった。

= This is the way I became happy.　（普通は how か the way のどちらか一方だけを使います）

❺ 関係代名詞を使った置き換え

関係副詞は前置詞の意味合いを併せ持っているので、《前置詞＋関係代名詞》で置き換えることができます。

where = in/on/at which　　　when = in/on/at which　　　why = for which

Finland is the country where I want to go.　フィンランドは私が行きたい国だ。

= Finland is the country to which I want to go.

I won't forget the day when my brother was born.　弟が生まれた日を私は忘れないだろう。

= I won't forget the day on which my brother was born.

**複合関係副詞**

❻ wherever：「…するところならどこでも」

You can sit wherever you want.　好きなところのどこにでも座っていいよ。

❼ whenever：「…するときはいつでも」

Visit me whenever you come to Kyoto.　京都に来るときはいつでも訪ねてきなさい。

# Pair Practice

1～5の年に起こったこととして正しい答えをa～fから選びましょう。そのあと下の会話例を参考にして、クラスメートと答え合わせをしましょう。

## Japanese History Quiz

| Year | Answer | What happened? |
|---|---|---|
| 例：1192 | b | a. The battle of Sekigahara occurred. |
| 1. 1600 | | b. The Kamakura Period began. |
| | | c. The Heian Period started. |
| 2. 1397 | | d. World War II ended. |
| | | e. Oda Nobunaga was killed by Akechi Mitsuhide. |
| 3. 794 | | f. The Golden Pavilion (Kinkaku-ji) was built. |
| 4. 1945 | | |
| 5. 1582 | | |

### 例

A: I think ( 1192 ) is the year when ( the Kamakura Period began ).
B: Yes, I think so, too. And (　　　　) is the year when (　　　　　　　　　　　).

# Unit 20　仮定法②：仮定法過去完了
## ▶ More Tips for Grammar ◀

仮定法過去完了は、過去の時点において事実でないことや実現の可能性がないことについて仮定的に述べるときに使います。

**基本形：《If ＋主語＋ had ＋過去分詞 , 主語＋ would / could ＋ have ＋過去分詞》「もし…だったら～だっただろうに」**

❶　if 節も主節も肯定文の場合

　　If I had studied harder, I could have passed the exam.　もっと熱心に勉強していたら、私は試験に受かることができただろうに。

　　If I had left home at 8:00, I could have arrived at Tokyo by noon.　8 時に家を出ていたら、私は正午までには東京に着けただろうに。

❷　if 節が否定文の場合：had → hadn't

　　If I hadn't eaten too much meat, I could have eaten cakes, too.　肉を食べ過ぎていなかったら、私はケーキも食べられたのになあ。

　　If it hadn't rained, we could have gone driving.　雨が降っていなかったら、ドライブに行けたのになあ。

❸　主節が否定文の場合：would / could → wouldn't / couldn't

　　If I had eaten enough meat, I wouldn't have eaten cake.　肉を十分食べていたら、ケーキを食べなかっただろうに。

　　If we had missed the train, we couldn't have participated in the tour.　その電車に乗り遅れていたら、私たちはツアーに参加できなかっただろう。

❹　if 節が後ろにくる場合

　　I would have cried if I had seen your face then.　あのときあなたの顔を見ていたら、私は泣いてたわ。

　　What would you have bought if you had won a lottery then?　あのとき宝くじが当たっていたら、あなたは何を買った？

**I wish を使った仮定法過去完了の表現**

❺　《I wish ＋主語＋ had ＋過去分詞》「…だったらよかったのに」

　　I wish I had gone grocery shopping yesterday.　昨日食料品の買い物に行っていたらよかったなあ。

　　I wish I hadn't seen the horror movie.　ホラー映画を見なければよかったなあ。

❻　《I wish ＋主語＋ could have ＋過去分詞》「…できたらよかったのに」

　　I wish I could have cooked dinner for you.　あなたに夕食を作ってあげられたらよかったんだけど。

**should を使った仮定法過去完了の表現**

❼　《should / shouldn't have ＋過去分詞》「…すべきだったのに／…すべきではなかったのに」

　　I should have slept more. I'm very sleepy.　もっと寝るべきだった。とても眠い。

　　I shouldn't have eaten too much at the party.　パーティーで食べ過ぎるんじゃなかった。

# Pair Practice

もし次の表内にあるような時代に生まれていたら、あなたはどのようなことをしていたと思いますか。自分の回答を書き、下の会話例を参考にしてクラスメートとシェアしましょう。

### If You Had Been Born in the....

|  | You | Partner |
|---|---|---|
| Heian Period |  |  |
| Edo Period |  |  |
| Jomon Period |  |  |
| Meiji Period |  |  |
| Sengoku Period |  |  |

A: What would you have done if you had been born in the ( Heian Period )?
B: I think ( I would have written a lot of poems ). How about you?

クラス用音声 CD 有り（別売）

# Grammar Network
コミュニケーションにリンクする英文法

2019 年 1 月 20 日　初版発行
2024 年 1 月 20 日　第 2 刷

著　者　稔本浩美、濱田真由美
発行者　松村達生
発行所　センゲージ ラーニング株式会社
　　　　〒102-0073　東京都千代田区九段北 1-11-11　第 2 フナトビル 5 階
　　　　電話　03-3511-4392
　　　　FAX　03-3511-4391
　　　　e-mail: eltjapan@cengage.com
　　　　copyright © 2019 センゲージ ラーニング株式会社

装　　丁　森村直美
組　　版　MAT（一ノ瀬湯夫）
本文イラスト　BURGEON／滝波裕子
印刷・製本　株式会社平河工業社

ISBN 978-4-86312-348-9

もし落丁、乱丁、その他不良品がありましたら、お取り替えいたします。
本書の全部または一部を無断で複写（コピー）することは、著作権法上での例外を除き、禁じられていますのでご注意ください。